The Wind
of Change

The Wind of Change

Harold Klemp

ECKANKAR
Minneapolis, MN

The Wind of Change

The terms ECKANKAR, ECK, EK, MAHANTA, SOUL TRAVEL, and VAIRAGI, among others, are trademarks of ECKANKAR, P.O. Box 27300, Minneapolis, MN 55427 U.S.A.

Printed in U.S.A.
ISBN: 0-88155-055-8
Library of Congress Catalog Card Number: 87-083647

Cover by Lois Stanfield
Cover photo by Pete Turner/The Image Bank
Ink Sketches by Diana Stanley

Fourth printing—1987

"It was always a low sound, deep and humming and seemingly a wind, a mighty rushing wind that passed somewhere in the distance, but never touched me."

—*The Tiger's Fang* by Paul Twitchell

Contents

Harold Klemp grew up on a Wisconsin farm. During his youth, he attended a two-roomed country schoolhouse before spending high school at a religious boarding school in Milwaukee, Wisconsin.

Following preministerial college in Milwaukee and Ft. Wayne, he enlisted in the Air Force. There he trained as a language specialist at the University of Indiana and a radio-intercept operator at Goodfellow AFB, Texas. Then followed a two-year stint in Japan where he first encountered Eckankar.

In October 1981, he became the present Mahanta, the Living ECK Master.

Introduction

ECK is the Wind of Change. It is that which sustains and perpetuates all Life in all of the universes. For those fortunate to have learned of Its existence, Life is an all-consuming adventure. Each day brings a new discovery.

That is what this book is about. The ECKist begins to analyze his life, and finally a pattern emerges—a golden thread—tying myriads of experiences and incidents together into a finale of Life.

For years Harold wondered how to put his ECK experiences down on paper so that others might benefit from them. As he says, "I let them percolate for a while." This book is the culmination of that percolation. It takes the reader back to the time when an ECKist just began to learn of the higher spiritual truths. If you are looking for a book that goes into long philosophical dissertations, this is not the one for you. The ECKist portrayed herein talks about everyday things, and how the ECK works and manifests in his life. You will travel with him from a farm in Wisconsin, to Japan, to Texas and into realms beyond all those places.

Today, people are asking, "How can Eckankar help me here, right now?" *The Wind of Change* is basically an answer to that question. It is a series of stories told with love and humor about how the ECK sustains and perpetuates the life and adventure of one man.

Marjorie Klemp

1

A Cow Tale

Before Eckankar came into my life, I so often wondered, "How much do I trust in God and how much must I do for myself?"

A story that helps answer this entails the camel driver who approached a wise man living on a desert oasis.

"Tell me," said the camel driver, "every night when I make camp, I can't decide whether to tie up my camel or to trust in God so it won't run away. What is right?"

The wise man said, "Let me contemplate on that tonight. Come back in the morning, and I'll give you the answer."

At sunrise the camel driver returned, bowed himself low before the wise man and awaited the solution to end his dilemma.

The wise man said, "The answer is this: Trust in God *and* tie up your camel!"

The camel driver was gratified at this wisdom and went his way in peace.

* * *

A cow on our farm once got herself in deep trouble with Dad. She could have used a little divine intervention. This happened on an early summer morning. The sun awoke to a crisp, cloudless sky promising a delightful day of cool weather for our farming community.

Dad and I had just finished milking the herd. He rinsed the last milker in hot water while I fed milk in a pail to several calves, and forked hay to the young heifers and the huge, black-and-white Holstein bull. Then I loaded the three milker machines onto the cart that already creaked under the weight of two cans of milk, and pushed the entire load over the gravel driveway to the milk house.

Meanwhile, Dad let the cows out of their stanchions in the barn so they could go out onto the barnyard. Lady, the farm dog, barked and snapped at their hooves to hurry them along.

I kept a watchful eye on the cows through the milk house window. The barnyard gate to the woods stood open. Most of the cows drank water from the tank right outside my window, then headed through the open gate and down the north lane to the day pasture by the woods.

One of the more adventurous cows lagged behind by a closed gate. It blocked off a field of luscious, green night pasture behind the barn. She gazed wistfully over the oak gate, admiring the bountiful acres of delicious salad tempting her from the other side.

The new oak gate was Dad's pride. He had made it from sturdy lumber, laying the wood out on the lawn and piecing it together lovingly with hammer and saw.

"Just let them try to climb over *that!*" he grunted, driving the last nail.

4

The temptation of the forbidden tall grass proved too strong for the Holstein cow. While I returned to washing milkers and Dad fed pigs, she heaved her burly black-and-white chest against the gate, testing

The cow was in serious trouble. I heard the tractor roar to life...

its strength. Not impressed, she started to climb over. A loud, cracking noise of splintering boards tore the air as the once-sturdy oak gate crashed under the weight of the cow.

Dad heard the crashing sound from the pig barn and knew immediately what it meant. He released a volley of shouts, several insane screams, then bolted toward the barn with the dog barking excitedly in his tracks.

The cow was in serious trouble. I heard the tractor roar to life where it was parked deep in the bowels of the barn. Dad raced it recklessly outside toward the cow. Lady, the dog, got to the cow first and snapped at her heels. The cow lumbered along further into the tall grass, reluctant to desert her succulent paradise, no matter the horrendous consequences.

The tractor wheeled around the corner of the barn in heated pursuit of the cow. Dad was furious. His shouts rang in the air, the tractor snorted, the dog howled, and the cow bellowed. The cavalcade moved swiftly down the long field toward a huge drainage ditch that bordered the north edge of the pasture. The cow led the chase by a tail.

Dad's intention was to teach the cow a dear lesson and run her within a breath of her life. Her gait had slowed considerably by the time she neared the far end of the pasture.

Through the milk house window, I watched the spectacle of the cow's flight in fascination. Divine intervention seemed the only possible solution to her problem.

By this time my sympathy was with the cow, even though she had crumpled Dad's special gate. I felt her punishment was enough, but the chase continued without abatement. Dad bumped her flying hooves with the tractor's front tires. With the tractor nipping her heels and the impassable ditch yawning darkly before her nose, the cow seemed to face certain disaster.

Just when it seemed she must plunge into the deep ditch to elude her relentless pursuers, the cow turned left, sharply left. She dug her hooves into the dew-covered sod right at the brink of the ditch and pulled a square jerk to the left.

That maneuver startled Dad. He had no time to turn. The tractor wheels skidded on the wet grass, brakes locked, in a desperate, but futile attempt to avoid the ditch. Dad and the tractor dipped silently out of sight behind the ditch bank.

I left my observation post at the window and ran for the car in the garage. Mother raced out of the house.

"Dad's in the ditch!" I shouted through the car window as I raced off to help. Both Dad and the tractor had disappeared completely from view. I feared the worst.

Dad's violent anger had gotten him into trouble more than once. Now, perhaps, he was dead.

Lady stood like a silent sentinel on the brim of the ditch, sadly studying the puzzling scene below. The cow tossed her head with disdain as she trotted back to the barnyard. She had whipped the machine.

Dad's head emerged slowly over the top of the ditch.

7

Dad's head emerged slowly over the top of the ditch bank, a foolish grin plastered on his face. His untanned, bald head shone brilliantly in the sunlight. He retreated into the ditch to retrieve his ever-present straw hat. His rage had drowned itself someplace down there in the water and mud. The big tractor remained securely mired in the mud, too, tilted at a precarious angle.

Dad sent me home for our little tractor, but it was not strong enough to pull out the big tractor. Then Dad sent me for the pickup truck, but an elaborate scheme of the little tractor chained to the truck also failed to dislodge the entrenched vehicle.

Finally, Dad realized with despair that Aaron, our neighbor, would have to help pull with his *giant* tractor. This entailed an explanation of sorts to Aaron. Aaron kept a sober face as he surveyed the half-buried tractor lying in the mud. Dad sheepishly pretended there was nothing at all so strange about a tractor stuck in a ditch. My guess, nonetheless, was that this was a "first" in the history of our community.

Aaron's giant tractor pulled our big tractor out as easily as a toy. Aaron waved genially as he roared home again, the sober expression still cheerfully locked on his face.

It is difficult to guess whether or not the cow thought to ask for a miracle in her predicament. I did notice, however, that without waiting for an answer, she promptly turned the corner. She had as much sense as the wise man on the desert oasis.

2

Animal Heaven

Do animals have a heaven? What do you suppose? I know they do. Animals also have a definite state of consciousness like you or I. That is because they are Souls, too. Perhaps their unfoldment has not yet reached the human level, but their incarnation is an important step toward God Consciousness.

One has to know and love animals to even care whether or not they will live after they have shed their physical bodies. One of my good friends on the farm was a mother cat named Zsa Zsa.

Zsa Zsa was a devoted mother with gray-and-white fur. She proved diligent in raising and training her annual litter of kittens. She did not idly lie around the farm, but nursed and played with her little ones.

Moreover, when the kittens were big enough to walk well and mind her mewing commands, Zsa Zsa took them into the cornfield or the oats field to show them how to survive in the wilds.

For days at a time, she and the kittens disappeared on these hunting trips. We kids were sad about that because generally if she left home with

9

four kittens, she often returned with only three. The missing one was a sacrifice to the harsh laws of survival in nature.

Our farm cats did not have to hunt for food unless they wanted to. They got plenty of food scraps from our dinner table as well as milk during milking chores.

Kenner, a shrewd tomcat, would sit patiently in the center alley of the barn waiting for Dad or me to empty the milk machine buckets into the pail. Then he would enthusiastically lick up the milk that accidentally splashed onto the concrete floor. When Kenner thought nobody was watching, that dear old lazy, but crafty cat would ease himself up comfortably close to the pail and steal a few hearty licks from it of that oh-so-good and warm, fresh milk straight from the cow.

Kenner was often the father of Zsa Zsa's kittens. The difference between Kenner and Zsa Zsa as parents was striking. She was industrious, out hunting mice for her family so they might develop their

He would ease himself close to the pail.

latent hunting skills. Kenner, on the other hand, would sit lazily by the milk pail watching for scattered drops of milk to soothe his hunger pangs. He had the disposition of a shiftless alley cat.

Although fourteen cats roamed our farm and most of them became my friends, Zsa Zsa remained special. She had lost her back right leg to a muskrat trap when she was no more than a large kitten. Dad had carelessly set the trap in the corn crib to catch a bursting population of rats and caught Zsa Zsa by mistake.

I heard Zsa Zsa's terrible cry that morning. Her leg was caught in the merciless jaws of the trap. I ran out to the mulberry tree on the front lawn where Dad was holding the trap up by the chain. The yowling Zsa Zsa dangled helplessly from the other end. When the jagged jaws finally released their vicious bite, she scooted under the granary to hide. Her heart-rending cries sounded most of the day. I wondered if she would live.

The other cats tried to console her, but in her blinding pain Zsa Zsa bared her teeth and unsheathed her claws. They retreated and left her alone.

Zsa Zsa was her own doctor. She gnawed off the splintered bone until it was tight against where her fur still grew undamaged. In time, only dried bone protruded from what had once been her healthy leg.

From then on, she became a common sight around the farm as she displayed her awkward hop. But when my little sister brought the food scraps out at noon to feed the cats, Zsa Zsa pushed her way to a prime position at the food tray. Even Lady, the farm dog, gave her plenty of room. Zsa Zsa was a firm, tough lady—missing leg or not.

11

She soon became one of my favorite farm friends. She would hop into the woodshed as I chopped kindling for the kitchen stove or split blocks of wood into smaller chunks to fit the wood furnace in the basement.

Zsa Zsa climbed up on the woodpile to watch, safely out of range from accidental missiles splintering

Zsa Zsa climbed up on the woodpile to watch.

off the blocks of wood that caromed wildly at times around the woodshed. She knew that soon I would tire of splitting wood and sit down to rest. The smell of the cookie in my shirt pocket further invited her patience.

Finally, I would set the axe down and wipe the sweat from my forehead. My shirt was hanging from a nail over the door, the cookie in the top left pocket. I pulled it out and broke it in two so it would last a little longer. Zsa Zsa ate it contentedly in my lap, finished, then peered expectantly into my face. Would I please get another cookie from the house?

I shook my head. No more cookies. She carefully jumped from my lap, reached back up to my cheek and planted a couple of "thank you" licks on my nose, then disappeared out of the woodshed door with her peculiar hop.

Just about this time, Uncle Sam beckoned with his long finger. I enlisted in the Air Force rather than face the army's inevitable draft notice for Viet Nam. After training, the Air Force sent me overseas to Japan.

When I returned two years later, I hardly expected that Zsa Zsa would remember me. After all, somebody else had fed her while I was gone. Would not her loyalty be to whoever fed her?

I was pleased when Zsa Zsa hopped out of the barn to greet me. Her gray and white fur was still silky and clean, befitting a lady of her position. She was still the queen of the cats. I scooped her up into my arms. Zsa Zsa meowed softly, lovingly, saying how glad she was to see me again. She purred and licked my face, her rough tongue washing my cheeks, nose and chin with great affection.

Suddenly, Zsa Zsa struggled to get out of my arms. I let her down to the ground. She seemed intent on some important errand that beckoned. Quickly, she disappeared into the tall grass behind the machine shed.

I continued walking around the farm, indulging myself in the rural sights and sounds that had been so far out of reach during my two years overseas.

Dad had not been able to keep the farm buildings in repair as well as when his four sons were still at home. We had all been gone for some time now, three in the military and another married. Routine farm chores had tied up his day. He used to keep the machinery and buildings in repair while we did the evening chores. But I was home now to help out. Things would be different, better.

A soft meow broke into my thoughts. Zsa Zsa stood at my feet with a freshly caught mouse in her mouth. I was her Prodigal Son, one of her many kittens come home. She showed no prejudice in matters of the heart. Zsa Zsa loved me like one of her own.

Gently, she laid the field mouse at my feet. I knelt down, quite overcome by emotion, and softly stroked her gleaming fur.

She meowed again, looking expectantly into my eyes as if to say: "Go ahead, eat it! I got it just for you! This is your coming-home present!" For once, I declined a gift of love.

Zsa Zsa died a short time later. If there is, however, one thing I know, there is a heaven for cats like her. Perhaps even for that dear old lazybones, Kenner.

3

A Question of Salvation

A most startling revelation came to me late one night while I was preministerial student in a Protestant college. This gave a spiritual jolt that revamped my outer life in preparation for later stepping onto the path of ECK.

It was during this particular spiritual crisis that I so strongly felt the firm touch of the ECK, or Spirit, in my spiritual worlds, forcing me to drop the ministry as a future profession.

The evening that led to this spiritual shock started ordinarily enough. Our dorm softball team had just lost a game in the intramural league. The catcher and I rehashed the errors and silent bats that had contributed to the loss. But presently the topic veered toward more philosophical matters.

Our session concluded about one o'clock in the morning. I fretted about an upcoming test scheduled for the first hour, wishing now I had spent more time at the study desk.

Don, the catcher, remained unruffled. "Mine's multiple choice," he yawned. "I can fake it." The stocky catcher stumbled wearily out of the study room and disappeared into his bedroom to recline in the soothing and guileless cradle of sleep.

Our talk had ranged over a wide variety of religious "what if's," leaving me in a high state of mind. I noted a surprising clarity of mind begin to envelop me. I fervently wished for someone to join me here in the downstairs lounge in order to continue this probe into the religious unknown.

I wondered, for instance, do only Christians go to heaven? Is there more than one heaven? If so, which religious group goes to the highest one? If only Christians go to heaven, what is the fate of the heathen? From religion class, I recalled St. Paul

I wondered, for instance, do only Christians go to heaven?

speaking of a man he had known fourteen years earlier who had been caught up even to the third heaven. Why did we know so little about heaven? I wanted to know more.

I sat down on the couch to ponder this. The lounge had two large windows facing the sidewalk outside. This was a small church college, and nearly all the students knew each other. Friendliness pervaded the campus. If anyone was out walking at this late hour, he would surely drop in for hospitality's sake. But no one did.

The fireplace stood cold and empty. I sat huddled up for warmth, too keyed up to sleep. Finally, with nothing else to do and the morning test drawing ever closer, I went up to bed.

But for a long time, sleep refused to come. I listened to the slow, heavy breathing of my roommate coming from his single bed along the opposite wall. Finally, I fell into a light sleep. My breathing deepened. It still seemed possible to catch a few hours of rest before dawn.

A peculiar thing occurred then. I was lying on my bed, face toward the ceiling. My Spiritual Eye opened and I saw the most incredible sight. Beautiful, white, fluffy clouds scattered themselves across an effervescent blue sky. The clouds parted and a fortress appeared. The fortress was of the old style, a remnant left over from the hoary, biblical days of Jericho. Its walls looked high and formidable, constructed not of rubies and diamonds or other heavenly gems, but of sturdy, gigantic blocks of stone. Facing in my direction stood the mighty portals, the only entrance to this bastion.

The scene startled me, although I was not afraid. I had an intense curiosity to find out what this was all about. Then a voice spoke.

17

A soft man's voice, tinged with a Southern accent, said, "You will see and know what no man has ever seen and known before." Years later, I recognized the voice at the 1969 ECK Seminar in Los Angeles as that of Paul Twitchell, the Living ECK Master, founder of the modern-day teachings of Eckankar.

The voice repeated the sentence. When it finished, the two giant gates slowly began to part. I did not know that the message meant insight into my own spiritual worlds. Like so many people who have visions, I thought the message was for everybody.

As the gates slowly continued to open, my mind raced ahead to evaluate the message from the voice. An instant later, it computed an answer that put me into another kind of shock.

"If this information is truly so great and special," whispered my mind, "doesn't it stand to reason it might also kill you?"

Frantically I shouted at the doors, "No, no! I don't want to see and know *anything!*"

The doors stopped. They began to close. The whole vision disintegrated, the colors faded, the vision fled.

The next instant, I found myself back on the bed, legs slung over the edge, feet planted firmly on the floor. I was badly shaken and thoroughly soaked with sweat.

"Good grief," I thought, "I'm not ready to die."

How true. The thought of death petrified me. Somehow, through all my religious indoctrinations, I had not accumulated any confidence in the afterlife. I felt like the man who confessed with heartfelt earnestness, "Sure, I want to go to heaven, but not if I have to die to get there!"

Dan, my roommate, slept on contentedly. For what seemed like hours, I was too scared to go to sleep. Only when the first soft washes of dawn began to splash across the black night sky did I catch a quick catnap.

I stayed in shock most of the morning. I took the test, apparently, but I do not remember. But I did not go to the main chapel with the rest of the students at ten o'clock. Our dorm had a little, one-man chapel in the basement suited especially for a situation like mine.

I stepped into the small room that was hardly more than a closet. A cushioned kneeler stood in front of a miniature altar. I dropped onto the kneeler and began to pray earnestly for comfort and help from Christ. After all, that was my life. But no help came. In fact, just the opposite happened, Christ was cut off from my spiritual life entirely.

It happened like this. I found myself in the Soul body, hovering over the earth. As I floated like a pair of eyes, I was conscious of a religious umbilical cord that trailed away from me into the outer reaches of space. That cord was the lifeline that supplied my religious inclinations. To my horror, somebody cut it with a golden scissors. The severed cord floated away and disappeared into the black oblivion of space. Perplexed and terrified, I began to wonder if there was indeed a stronger spiritual force in my life than Christ.

A short while later, I returned to the physical body. I found myself draped over the little kneeler in front of the altar as before. Tears of immense sorrow burst from my eyes. I had not cried in years. Finally, I dried my eyes and returned to class.

The vision was gone. I was left to survey the shattered ruins of years of religious training. A change had swept through me though I was not to recognize its deep-lying impact for many months.

The aimlessness of my preministerial studies stood out in stark relief. I now knew that a key element was missing from the heart of all my religious education. This was the first step toward Eckankar.

4

My Own Laws and the Air Force

"Stir it! Stir it! I don't want no lumps!" The burly Air Force sergeant hovered over me in the squadron hobby shop. I stirred the mustard-yellow paint still more briskly.

This was the Air Force in early 1965. Basic training was done. Most of the sixty or so airmen in my training flight had already received their orders to various military technical schools or air bases across the nation. Nearly all of my old friends had shipped out.

Those of us awaiting specialized orders were transferred to the graduate barracks. The airmen in this barracks were leftovers from a number of other graduated flights, and they also awaited orders. My orders had not come through yet for the choice assignment of Russian language school at Indiana University.

The orderly room, in the meantime, sent us out on lowly squadron details in order to earn our keep. This week, the detail clerk sent me to the hobby shop, a nice name for squadron maintenance.

Sergeant Bandy watched me closely from the carpenter's bench that served as his desk. He sat in a wooden barrel chair, the two front legs tipped back off the floor as he relaxed with his feet on the bench. A hot cup of breakfast coffee stood within easy reach, two jelly-filled doughnuts alongside the steaming cup.

"Keep it up! No lumps!" he badgered. I stirred until my arms ached. As long as I stirred the paint, the sergeant could putter aimlessly at his breakfast and not be bothered with finding constructive work for me. I was assigned here all week long. I wondered how long I would last. Where were my orders to the paradise of the civilian university, away from dehumanizing brutes like this Sergeant Bandy?

Fifteen minutes later, he plopped his feet back onto the floor, shot me a sour glance as he brushed the crumbs from the bench. "Now paint the tool shed," he growled. Sergeant Bandy was a sly old devil of a sergeant who had made the squadron hobby shop his nest. Here he hoped to serve out the

I started to brush paint into the cracks.

remaining years before retirement. He was the squadron's handyman, dabbling with rough carpentry, a little plumbing, a little of a lot of things.

I picked up the bucket of mustard-colored paint and a floppy brush, then retreated out of the shop and just around the corner where he could not watch me. I started to brush paint into the cracks, wishing for a new assignment in tomorrow's detail roster. Finally, later that afternoon, the little tool shed bore a dubious coat of fresh, murky-yellow paint.

Sergeant Bandy saw that I was done. "Come on in here," he shouted. "Clean up the brush. I've got something else for you."

I could not find any cleaning rags.

"Sure, I know where there are rags," he croaked. Thrusting a pudgy finger out of the doorway, he pointed to a clothesline alongside the neighboring barracks. "See over there?"

I got the picture. He expected me to calmly steal a bed sheet, come back and tear it up for rags. It did not take much to see that this was a "can't win for losing" proposition. The airmen in the barracks were out training, but every barracks always posted a guard. If he spotted me, the Air Police would immediately extend an invitation to the guardhouse. This would also cancel my orders to language school.

I debated how to salvage the situation. The old sergeant's word would be taken before mine in a military court. If I claimed he ordered me to take the sheet, he would deny it, of course. After all, why risk his retirement benefits?

"Well, you get yourself a couple of rags off that line," he said with a wave of his hand.

As the old saying goes, I was caught between the devil and the deep blue sea. But I balked. There was no way I would steal clothes off that line. Believe me, the power of a sergeant's suggestion is overwhelmingly strong right after basic training. When a sergeant orders you to do something, you do it without question.

My feet stayed rooted to the floor. If the barracks guard spotted me, Sergeant Bandy would back off and say he knew nothing about the scheme. I was scared and shook inside.

"No, sir."

The old sergeant whirled around, aghast at my defiance. "What?" he shrieked.

"I won't do it!"

Sergeant Bandy scolded, cursed, and threatened, but my legs were not moving toward the clothesline. Finally, he gave up.

Until then, I had revered men with superior rank. This was a serious defect in my character. I have since learned that one must earn the respect of others. This sly, old sergeant certainly did not belong on the pedestal where I had so indiscriminately placed him along with all other sergeants. Somehow, I thought he would know better about not stealing.

This incident happened three years before I found Eckankar. But even then, the agelong lessons of *karma*, the Law of Cause and Effect, had been deeply instilled in me. I knew the decision was mine alone whether or not to steal. I also knew instinctively that some unseen law would demand payment for every infraction.

For the remainder of the week, the detail assignment placed me back in Sergeant Bandy's hobby shop. Bandy lost no opportunity to find the most distasteful tasks for my torment, and his pleasure. But never again did he tell me to steal.

Next Monday morning, I got up the courage to ask the detail sergeant to please give me any assignment but the hobby shop. He understood. Apparently, Sergeant Bandy had made his reputation a long time ago. I found myself out of the clutches of that old scoundrel forever.

Not long after that, the long awaited orders came for language school. I shuddered when I considered how close I had let myself come to the guardhouse.

5

The Good-Rumor Man

I lingered in the graduate barracks with airmen from other graduated training flights who also awaited their orders. We all wished desperately to ship out and get as many miles as possible between us and Lackland Air Force Base in Texas. But most of us were expecting specialized orders, and they took longer.

The grad barracks was thus the house of busted dreams. Daily we longed for word of our departure. We all wanted a more substantial education than the squadron's dirty work. Some of us had been promised nine months of intensive language training in Russian, Chinese, German, or one of a number of other tongues.

We had long since become suspicious of the promises made by military desk clerks that our assignments to Syracuse University or Indiana University would be in tomorrow, and surely, no later than the day after that.

And yet, the adage "no news is good news" soon wears thin. Especially in the military where each of us feared the whim of some desk clerk who might put his pencil to paper and magically transfer us to cook school or to the Air Police.

Every morning the forty of us trudged off to our respective details, then stumbled home again at night to learn which of the tech schools were opening new classes and had sent orders to our barracks residents. Usually, the news was the same—none.

One Tuesday in the chow hall, a heartening rumor circulated among the bedraggled members of our grad barracks. "Hey," said Rick, "I heard Syracuse University is getting a batch of language airmen. Maybe that's us!"

"Who told you that?" I asked suspiciously, not allowing the tenderness of hope to rise too high within my chest.

"A couple of the boys were talking about it at the next table."

I forked down my pile of scrambled eggs, alternating them with mouthfuls of nicely browned toast. Language training at a university was a choice assignment. I did not want to believe any unfounded rumors, but it sure made me happy to think the day of my departure from Lackland was probably just around the corner. This was a most pleasant and happy thought to carry along on another day of seemingly endless squadron details.

Nothing came of the rumor, but several others quickly followed. A few days later when our spirits had lagged again, Nick said to me on the way to the Airmen's Club after work, "Say, I hear Syracuse is opening up another class and so is Indiana!"

"No kidding," I said. I was catching on to the spirit of this good news. But I was curious about the source. Who was bothering to lift our spirits by implanting light, gentle rumors through the grad barracks?

I asked Nick, "Did you hear that in the orderly room?"

Nick was a great believer in hovering around the orderly room. In fact, he usually wrangled a job there. His dad, a former army man, had told him to get to the nerve center of the squadron—the orderly room—if he wanted to know the latest military scuttlebutt, like upcoming orders.

"Yes," he said, "not officially, but Ray told me. We were both detailed to the orderly room today. He overheard the squadron clerk on the phone."

The picture of the rumor-spreader was coming into focus. Several times now, Ray's name had turned up in connection with the happy rumors. Was Ray the Rumor Man?

I knew Ray slightly. He had moved into the grad barracks about the same time as I had. Ray had been in our sister flight under that demon, Sergeant Sharp. Sharp drove his men through a most exacting and exasperating—infuriating—training program, a relic of the Second World War.

But Ray had survived. However, the grueling discipline had left a scratch on his wry sense of humor, sharpening it considerably.

When the newest rumor circulated among the men after the first two still lacked fruition, I approached Ray.

"What's this I hear that language airmen are going to live in civilian dorms at the universities?"

"Shhh," he cautioned, glancing quickly over his shoulder to avoid eavesdroppers. "Can you keep a secret?"

"Sure," I whispered, "what's the story?"

The lean, tall Texan leaned over and drawled a conspiratorial whisper. "Only the Russian language

29

airmen get the civilian dorms—and only at Indiana."

"What else?"

"This is just a rumor, but no inspections, passes every weekend, and we can wear civilian clothes to class."

"Fantastic!" I breathed. "Where did you hear all this?"

"I made it up," Ray said with a hurt look on his face. "You don't really think all those good things could happen, do you?"

"But why?"

"I'm spreading happiness rumors. They lift the morale of the boys. It's more fun in here with everyone happy than moping around tense and afraid they'll end up in cook school."

"There's nothing to the rumors?" My disappointment must have showed, for Ray was quick to lift my morale.

"Oh, sure," Ray said, "we're keeping positive, and the rumors have got to happen."

The happy rumors continued to circulate around the barracks. I disregarded them, of course, since I knew the source, but I now studied the effect they had upon the attitudes of the other airmen. Nobody seemed to care that so far none had come true. The satisfaction of hope made each day a little brighter and happier.

Ray continued his undercover work of inventing the most uplifting rumors that he could spin from the fabric of his imagination. He became our unsung and unknown Morale Sergeant. His job ended the day our orders finally arrived for Russian language training at Indiana University. He had carried us through.

When we arrived there two months later, many of the rumors proved unfounded. For one thing, airmen lived in barracks at the Air Force detachment near campus, not in civilian dorms. But the barracks were *like* dorms, except that our housemother was a chubby sergeant.

We *did* have inspections, contrary to early rumors. There were *no* passes *every* weekend, but we had the run of the campus town and a radius of perhaps 100 miles. This gave us a great deal more freedom than a pass, because weekend passes were dished out begrudgingly elsewhere in the Air Force.

Civilian clothes for classes were *out*, military uniforms *in*. But after class, we could slip into our civilian clothes to eat at the campus cafeteria and snack down at the student union.

Thus the rumors were not accurate in the way of our thinking, but the overall picture at the university far surpassed any of our wildest dreams.

Ray had kept our spirits at a high level during the depression period in the grad barracks. Outside of myself, I doubt whether any of the other airmen remembered or cared about those rumors back at Lackland. That was just a past life and better forgotten.

Ray and I later became good friends. I thought it wise to cultivate the friendship of a Good-Rumor Man. Who knows when again I might need one?

6

Footnote from the Good-Rumor Man

One evening as Ray, my Air Force friend, and I munched hamburgers in the student union, I reflected upon all the rumors he had initiated back at Lackland Air Force Base in Texas. I asked him about the nature of rumors in celestial matters.

"Do you suppose any of the rumors are true about heaven?"

"What rumors?" he asked.

"Oh, you know, the halos, the wings, the eternal rest, and all that,"

"I don't know about them," he said upon reflection, but I heard there's no eternal hell...."

I pushed back from the table, picked up my tray and headed for the kitchen window to deposit the dirty dishes. Ray followed with his tray.

"And I suppose," I reflected, "that the wings are gilded, the halos of gold, and no sergeants?"

"Oh, very true," Ray assured me.

"And, do rumors get beyond the celestial gates?"

"Some, I suppose," he answered with his slow Texas drawl. "Yes, I suppose the good ones."

"Well, if you're going, you can count me in," I said. "Heaven sounds like a really happy place."

"That's the rumor," say Ray earnestly. I smiled. Once a Good-Rumor Man, always a Good-Rumor Man.

Several years were still to pass before I would read Paul Twitchell's *The Tiger's Fang*, an account of the various heavens as traveled by the great ECK Adept in the company of the Tibetan, Rebazar Tarzs. Later, I used the book as a road map, visiting many of those very same heavens via Eckankar and the Ancient Science of Soul Travel.

The Good-Rumor Man and I walked the dark streets in meditative silence before slowly returning to the barracks for the night.

7

Weather or Not

Sometime during Soul's long sojourn in the worlds of matter, energy, space and time, It gets to play with all sorts of meaningless phenomena of nature. This is generally a detour from Its most direct efforts to God-Realization.

Perhaps I had gained the ability to manipulate the weather in some other, long-forgotten era when I, as Soul, roamed the earth in a primitive body. The ECK, or Spirit, is the best guide when one gathers information in these arts. The training by the Living ECK Master insures that once one has learned all there is to know about the subject, the Living ECK Master is there to drag him out of trouble by the ears, if deemed necessary.

I have always experienced an aversion to military ceremonies. Functions such as parades, inspections, and retreat are carried out in order to develop tight discipline within a military organization. This is a good procedure — for somebody else. I especially disliked retreat.

Retreat is the flag-lowering ceremony usually held at the end of the day. A flight of sixty airmen assembled in the squadron parking lot after the day shift and marched out to the flagpole. Here they solemnly watched two other airmen lowering the Stars and Stripes while a bugler played the sad notes.

It is true, somebody had to bring in the flag, and to that I certainly had no objections. I did object that I was to be one of the sixty airmen who merely stood by and watched. The flag was not heavy. Two men were more than enough to carry it from the flagpole.

Retreat was assigned on a rotating basis to all the squadrons at Yokota Air Base in Japan. Each squadron pulled retreat only once every few weeks. Since our squadron consisted of several hundred men, retreat came seldom enough. I should hardly have resented the duty.

But I did. I set up such an inner opposition to it that the weather took pity and rained each and every day I was to stand retreat. Time after time, during the period of more than a year that I was assigned to Yokota, my retreat ceremonies were cancelled by downpours.

None of the airmen on the shift noticed this until a few days before I shipped out back to the States. Then Hubert, an intelligent and perceptive airman assigned to today's retreat from our squadron, looked puzzled and remarked in passing, "Say, don't you ever stand retreat?"

"No," I said smugly, "as a matter of fact, I don't. Mine have all been rained out." I let out my secret to Hubert because I felt safe with my imminent return to the States.

My older brother, who preceded me through the Air Force, had given me a single bit of valuable advice that I had now forgotten in my smugness: "If you've got a good thing going, don't tell anybody— especially your best friend!"

36

With a sinking feeling in my stomach, I realized what my brother had meant. Hubert shouted out to the other members on our shift, "Hey, Harry's never stood retreat and he's going back to the States! Can't we help him out?"

Until then I thought myself safe, since I had my final orders in hand. Only a lot of fast talking and throwing myself upon their everlasting friendship and goodwill succeeded in keeping my record unblemished. They did enjoy my discomfort immensely, however, during the moments when they debated whether or not to give me at least a taste of the squadron's retreat ceremony.

I do not know how I would have avoided retreat had I been stationed in the desert. Maybe the base would have suffered violent dust storms.

The next morning when I pulled out on the highway and headed west, the little thundercloud seemed to be waiting patiently for me to start driving again. Then it accompanied me west.

Perhaps a better way to say this is that I did not cause the rain at Yokota Air Base in Japan. The ECK, or Spirit, did—for Its own purposes. But I *knew* when it would rain, especially on the days I was slated for retreat.

At any rate, the refreshing rain has been a welcome companion to me on more than one occasion. And not just to get me out of something, but to refresh my travels. Years later, after my discharge from service and while I was driving leisurely for several days through the dry countryside of New Mexico, a small thunderstom preceded my journey well into Arizona.

The first night I stopped at a small New Mexico motel. A gas attendant at a nearby service station remarked on the thundershower overhead. "This is the first rain we've had in six months, since right before Christmas," he said, squinting his eyes skyward and shielding them from the rain with his cupped hand.

The next morning when I pulled out on the highway and headed west, the little thundercloud seemed to be waiting patiently for me to start driving again. Then it accompanied me west. I know nothing about the weather patterns for the Southwest, but it seemed more logical for the storm to be going east. I drove in the most refreshing coolness as the thundershower cooled the road before me all the way into Arizona.

Very often we do not really cause these phenomena of nature, but we are synchronized to see them when they do happen.

Lai Tsi, the great ECK Master in China, found that the SUGMAD, God, had the animals take care of him while he lay unconscious upon the cold floor of a cave high up in the hills of remote China.

The ECK, or Holy Spirit, still provides today. All it takes is the eyes to see, and the ears to hear. Even down to the simple, refreshing rain provided to a tired traveler by a friendly raincloud.

8

Soul Travel

Eckankar was about to come into my life. A great yearning grew inside me, but for what I did not know.

This was still Yokota Air Base in Japan. I had been stationed here for more than a year and often found myself homesick for the familiar countryside around our family farm back in the Midwest.

Metaphysical studies had increasingly caught my attention since I enlisted in the Air Force. Mystical studies had been a complete taboo previously while I struggled with orthodox dogmas as a preministerial student.

In those far-off college days, I began to seriously wonder what Soul was. What happened when a person died? Why did one individual leave the body with a happy smile touching the lips while another went out with the blind fury of a slaughtered animal? I had seen both.

Paul Twitchell addressed himself to the mysteries of Soul leaving the body. But that came later, in 1970, in a chapter of *Dialogues with the Master*.

But this was earlier, before Paul had published the book. Perhaps the unresolved questions about

Soul and death had caused my diligent search through so many occult subjects. Somebody had to have an answer.

The monotony of the daily military routine broke all at once during a two-week span when I stumbled across answers to metaphysical questions from three sources. I found literature on Edgar Cayce and the Rosicrucians. Here was insight into the subjects of *karma* and *reincarnation*. But the most helpful literature arrived after I answered a small ad by Paul Twitchell in *Fate* magazine. He offered to give instructions in Eckankar, the Ancient Science of Soul Travel.

When the ECK discourses arrived by mail, I told Willy, my best friend, about them. He was skeptical at best. Life for him consisted of wine, women, and song—in whatever order he chanced across them. That was the Here and Now for him. He trusted the scheme of life to take care of him when his time came to leave the earth. But he was curious all the same about my attempts at Soul Travel.

For a month and a half, I spent the suggested twenty minutes in contemplation at bedtime. This posed no problem, because I had no roommate just then and thus enjoyed a great deal of privacy and freedom.

Finally, one night, I found myself in the expanded consciousness, Soul Traveling. The Living ECK Master, Paul Twitchell at the time, appeared as a blue light and escorted me through the barriers of time and space back to the family farm in Wisconsin. He left me on my bed upstairs in our old farmhouse.

I could clearly hear the household sounds of Mother as she prepared the noon meal for Dad, who lay napping on the couch in the living room. After listening for several minutes to the unmistakable, familiar sounds downstairs, I returned to my bunk in Japan. A year later in 1968, Brad Steiger included this story in his biography of Paul Twitchell, *In My Soul I Am Free*, so I will not repeat the details here.

Back on my bunk in Japan, I sat up and rubbed my eyes. "Boy," I thought, "this Eckankar works! I'm going to tell Willy."

Although it was late at night I hopped out of bed, slipped on my shower clogs and padded across the hallway to Willy's room. Willy was passed out on his bunk—too much wine, women and song, but mostly wine. He proved beyond recall.

Here I stood with the greatest discovery of my life—that Soul exists and can do things—and the only one with whom I even dared share this news was oblivious to all physical sights and sounds. I trudged back into my room to wait for morning and a somewhat more sober audience.

When morning finally came, Willy listened to my account of Soul Traveling back to the States. His enthusiasm was understandably not overwhelming. After all, what did my experience do for him?

"It's like this," he concluded, shaking his carrot-topped head, "you Soul Travel, and I'll stick to what I know best—wine, women and song!"

Two years later, I dropped my studies of Edgar Cayce and the Rosicrucians—two otherwise, fine groups—but I saw they could take me no further.

Eckankar remains.

9

The Silver Cord

O ne of my early out-of-body experiences
occurred during the summer of 1968 while I was
stationed with the military at Ft. Meade, Maryland.

The barracks was nearly empty at ten o'clock
that Saturday when I turned in for the night. No
sooner had I shut my eyes and begun the Spiritual
Exercises of ECK than a strange humming sound
surrounded the bunk, swirling through my head like
a swarm of angry bees. The intensity of the buzzing
increased until I felt my body floating up and away
from the pillow.

"Can I really be floating?" I wondered. Opening
my eyes, I was startled to discover myself two feet
over the pillow. Only later did I realize that this was
an out-of-body adventure. Right then it felt like
some kind of physical levitation.

The humming sound subsided and I settled back
down on the bed. I did not want this phenomenon to
end. This floating in midair was one of the most
thrilling things I had ever encountered. And now it
was leaving just as mysteriously as it had come. The
adventure was over—or so I thought!

The instant my body had settled back down on

the bed, I tried to jump up and run to the next-door barracks to tell Sam, an Army buddy, who delved into occult subjects. But a huge spider web seemed to have entangled me helplessly upon the bed.

Gathering up every bit of determination, I struggled to the edge of the bed, somersaulted over the side onto the floor and suddenly found myself standing by the bedside, feeling incredibly light and happy.

Later I surmised that this out-of-body experience had started with the sound of buzzing bees and continued even as I rolled out onto the floor. Everything was so natural that it never dawned on me that as Soul, I had escaped the physical body and slipped into the next highest one, the astral body.

In *The Spiritual Notebook*, Paul Twitchell identifies the buzzing of bees as one of the sounds made by the ECK, or Spirit, on a certain inner plane.

Angrily, I leaned over to inspect the intruder. I was about to shake him by the shoulder when I realized with a start that the man asleep in bed was me! That was my physical body!

46

The bed sheets had spilled out onto the floor with my tumble, and I now bent down to scoop them up. But hidden beneath the sheets lay the first clue that I was out of the body. A pulsing, luminous cord resembling a plastic garden hose caught my eye. Its bluish-white glow brightened the dimly-lit room. The shining cord came from somewhere in the back of my head and trailed along the floor into the bed. Scanning the length of the luminescent cord from end to end, I was perplexed to see someone sleeping in my bed.

Angrily, I leaned over to inspect the intruder. I was about to shake him by the shoulder when I realized with a start that the man asleep in bed was me! That was my physical body!

Then I knew that the physical body slept while I observed it from the vantage point of Soul that had now clothed Itself in the astral form. This enlightenment amused me as I curiously studied the rumpled, sleeping body.

Its hair was tousled and the face had gone gray as it lay on its side in deep slumber. A certain lifelessness had stolen across the facial features. I was appalled at my mangy physical body resting so unperturbed while I scrutinized its blemishes objectively from the bedside.

My concentration was interrupted by the soft padding footsteps of someone approaching in the hallway. "This will be fun!" I thought. "Since I'm probably only an invisible ghost to anyone on the physical plane, I'll step in front of him so he'll have to walk right through me!"

But the visitor slipped into the room before I could even turn around, and he stationed himself in a dark corner by the dresser. The man stood at medium height and was of solid build. A distinguishing feature was his flashing blue eyes that calmly observed my movements.

The physical body continued to sleep soundly with me outside it, the glowing lifeline still joined the two bodies, the physical and the astral.

Sudden terror gripped me. The stranger's presence was frightening. Would he maliciously break the umbilical-like cord, killing the physical body?

Desperately I rushed at him, flailing both arms to drive him away. But the quiet stranger stopped my onrush with an invisible wall of energy that replaced the fear with serenity and warmth. My vision blurred, the room spun, and I lost consciousness.

Seconds later, when I reopened my eyes, I was back in my body. Soul was securely entrenched in the physical again. My relief was beyond description! But there was no sign of the stranger.

The only proof that something unusual had happened came the next morning when Sam dropped in before breakfast. He took me aside and confided that last night shortly after ten o'clock, a mysterious light had shown about him while he read in his room.

Sam claimed that he was shown a prophecy about his immediate future. When I told him my story, we were both deeply mystified.

Later, a year after my first Soul Travel experience to the farm in Wisconsin, and only a few weeks after my second experience in the barracks, I bought *In My Soul I Am Free* by Brad Steiger. On the cover was a picture of the stranger who had watched from the shadows. It was Paul Twitchell, the leader then of Eckankar. This was the first time I had physically seen his face.

The entire Soul Travel adventure, starting with the hum of buzzing bees until Paul Twitchell, the Living ECK Master at that time, put me back into the physical body, lasted no more than twenty minutes. But those were among the most startling and enlightening moments that ever shook my life.

Here was proof to me that I could survive outside my physical body and conquer the fear instilled by that haunting bugaboo called Death. In the Soul body, I am free!

10

The Deer Slayer

What can one say about karma, that spiritual cause-and-effect idea that sounds so familiar until somebody tries to demonstrate it by examples from his own life?

* * *

The first flurries of winter swirled down from the gray clouds, biting the lone hunter far below. In his right hand, the man clutched tightly a twelve-gauge shotgun.

He stood listening. The thick brush of the dense woods hid him from the two deer that moved cautiously along the frozen ground several hundred feet away. The hunter lifted his red cap from his head, the ear flaps uncovering his ears so that he could hear better.

"They're moving off to the north," he thought, as the deer swung around from behind him.

Then he, too, moved cautiously, following the occasional faint crackling of a broken branch or twig, sounds that marked the location of the fleeing deer.

The deer stopped, smelled the distinctive human

smell of their stalker as the wind switched behind him. The wind carried an odor of after-shave lotion, detergent and hair spray. To the deer, it was the stench of an intruder intent on killing them.

The hunter was the first to break from the woods into the open, plowed field. He dropped to his belly and carefully crawled underneath the barbed wire fence, pushing the shotgun slowly through ahead of him. Then he knelt down out of sight along the line fence, swung up the barrel and waited quietly. The deer, he reasoned, would continue to move along the deer trail that emerged from the woods several hundred feet to the west of him.

A slight rustle of dry leaves turned his attention toward the edge of the woods. A seven-point buck and a large doe stood almost invisible in the brush, scanning the open field ahead of them for danger. The hunter remained still, well-hidden.

The buck cleared the five-strand barbed wire fence with an easy leap, and the doe followed quickly

A seven-point buck and a large doe stood almost invisible in the brush....

like his shadow. The hunter eased back the hammer of the gun and sighted carefully along the blue-black barrel. Then he paused and cursed mildly, his eye leaving the bead of the front sight that was fixed directly on the buck's heart.

A third party, a yellow-coated hunter, had bumbled onto this little scene of life and death. He emerged from the woods farther down the line fence, beyond the two deer.

The deer stood directly in line between the two hunters. Neither could shoot without the risk of maiming the other, so both held fire.

Suddenly, both deer broke and ran across the large plowed field toward a rocky, tree-covered ledge several hundred yards further north. The first hunter, the closest, fired. The shotgun roared, and the buck stumbled but regained his feet. The doe stepped deliberately into the line of fire to make her body a shield for her mate.

The slug had apparently broken the buck's right front leg. The hunter's hurried shot fell low as he had miscalculated the rising grade along which the frantic deer fled.

The buck and doe now zigzagged, dodging the slugs from the shotguns of both hunters. They crashed into the brush on top of the limestone ledge. The far hunter had shot but once and missed high, as a spurt of sand puffed up alongside the distant ledge.

Breathlessly, the men ran toward each other.

"How come you missed?" shouted the one wearing the yellow jacket.

"You ought to be glad I did," retorted the other, who was clad in red. "My slug would have stuck you against that elm back there!"

"Well," grumbled the other, "they was too far off for me anyhow. Looks like you broke his leg though."

The conversation was harshly punctuated by a sudden barrage of shotguns exploding behind the wooded ridge where the deer had escaped.

"No use chasing them now," said the man in yellow. "They're somebody else's meat." He shrugged his shoulders in resignation.

The two men stared emptily toward the spot where the ringing shots had sounded, then turned and left by different trails.

The man in red, the stalker, paused a moment for reflection. He sensed that the inexorable Law of Life would someday exact full due from him for this injury to one of Its own, and the payment would be made upon demand at just the right moment.

The payment was to come due much later, and when it did, he was not expecting it. In the meantime, his life went on as always.

11

Till Spring

After my honorable discharge from the Air Force, I fell into a slow-paced routine of winter chores on our Wisconsin dairy farm. The work was hard, but satisfying. Still, I found it a great relief to know about Eckankar and Soul Travel. This put the spice of adventure into life.

Farm life was otherwise a pleasure, but the pleasure dimmed considerably whenever I pondered the relentless ritual of twice a day milking twenty-five high-kicking, fire-breathing, black-and-white Holstein cows.

Many was the time I edged gingerly with milking machine in hand into the stall of a particularly sprightly "kicker," only to fly out again the wink of an eye later.

The caroming milker duly followed me, skidding across the wide main alley into the opposite gutter. Within the same breath came the milker belt, but at a slightly higher elevation.

The milker belt was the strap used to hang the milker before the cow so impolitely discharged me from her stall.

Milking was followed by washing the milkers in an ice-encrusted water tank in the fountain house. Then came pig feeding. My own breakfast arrived last—four fried eggs, a pan full of bacon, and a good helping of toast. By eight o'clock, I had already earned it.

The next chore was cleaning the barn. The ingredients for this were simple—one tractor hitched to a manure spreader, one shovel, and one farmer.

It leaves me astounded to see what a huge pile of manure a herd of twenty-five cows can produce in a single day. I loaded cow manure by hand every morning, seven days a week, in sunshine or in storm, in sickness or in health.

This soon inspired a dreadful longing for spring. Then the cows would return to pasture and fertilize the fields directly, without my slavish, shovel-wielding intervention.

Spring does not come fast under these conditions. It seems to poke along forever.

The rest of the winter routine ran on this order: barn cleaned by eleven o'clock in the forenoon, then an hour and a half of miscellaneous chores. Next, dinner at noon.

The afternoons passed by making wood for the kitchen stove and basement furnace, periodically bagging twenty bags of dusty oats, and shoveling up half a truckful of corn in the frigid corn crib outside. This grain was all ground together at the mill in town for cow feed, pig feed or chicken feed.

As the winter sun started to slide behind the woods far to the west, I would climb up into the thirty-foot silo and chip loose enough pieces of frozen silage with a dirt pick in order to satisfy the voracious appetites of all those hungry cows, plus fifteen heifers, and that big, mean bull.

After that, I was content to retreat into the house for warmth from the kitchen stove and a hot supper.

The final effort of the day came in pushing back from the generously laden supper table, buttoning up my lined barn jacket, and trudging out through the snow and blowing wind toward the barn for evening milking.

The same hostile herd of high-kicking, nasty, tail-switching Holsteins stretched their lightning-fast hind legs in avid anticipation of when I would try to hang the milker under their enormous stomachs.

A three-star cow boasted a kick that deposited the milker, milk belt, and me, plus any stray cat, into the aisle with a single smooth, blindingly fast motion.

The herd was probably as bored with the long, harsh winter as anyone. These four-legged outlaws developed their odd sense of humor during milking time. It kept their spirits high until spring released them from the stanchions that imprisoned them throughout the winter. They carefully honed their humor to a fine point on me.

These renegades seemed to place wagers on which kicker could shoot the milker, the milk belt, and me closest to the manure-filled gutter across the alley.

Through fitful observation, I speculated on the rules of their sport. A cow earned one point for merely dislodging the milker and sending it into the alley. The two-point kicker could deliver both the milker and the milk belt into the alley. A three-star cow boasted a kick that deposited the milker, milk belt, and me, plus any stray cat, into the aisle with a single smooth, blindingly-fast motion.

The latter performance drew a standing ovation from the entire herd. All other cows arose and chorused out the most deafening roar of approving moos. The victory of beast over man.

The champion also netted extra silage and grist that her obliging neighbors pushed along in the trough with their noses from their own portions.

After milking this gauntlet of high-kicking, fire-spitting Holsteins morning and night, all week long, in sunshine and in storm, sickness or in health— well, I was ready for spring.

Although milking continued all year, the cows seemed to walk off a lot of their extra steam in spring and summer when they ran the pasture. Hence, fewer of their magnificent kicks.

How did I endure until the April showers and May flowers? Believe me, it took more than just the far-off promise of spring. Each night after chores, I settled gladly into bed for relaxation. I came to appreciate this quiet time and contemplated with the Spiritual Exercises of ECK. Eckankar and Soul Travel provided a refreshing kind of *high* adventure into the far-flung inner universes. That was a delightful change from the overabundance of *low* adventure during milking.

Why would anyone try something so exotic as Soul Travel on a dairy farm? In my case, it helped me get to spring.

If you doubt me, spend a frigid winter yourself on a farm stocked with twenty-five wild Holsteins, fifteen heifers, one enormous and vicious bull, forty squealing hogs, and three hundred cackling hens.

You might try Soul Travel, too—at least, till spring!

12

The ECK-Vidya

Dreams into the future have always held a peculiar fascination for me. "Wouldn't it be great," I so often mused, "if I could see in dreams all that's going to happen in the future?"

This was the ideal, my secret dream of dreams. Eventually, an answer came to quench this thirst. It was spoken on the inner planes by Paul Twitchell, who was the Living ECK Master when I was still on the farm.

The insight came one night as I went up to my bedroom to do the Spiritual Exercises of ECK. I walked up the icy stairway to our ancient farmhouse and creaked along the rubber-matted wooden steps.

Next, I pulled a quilt from the bed, placed the fluffy pillow on the floor for a seat, and snuggled into the cozy quilt for warmth.

Immediately, I shut my eyes and put the attention on a blank imaginary screen in the area of the Spiritual Eye, a point just above the eyebrows in the center of the forehead. Gently, then, I started to chant the word *HU*, one of the ancient names for God. It sounds like the name "Hugh," except that it is chanted softly in a long, drawn-out breath.

"HU-U-UUU," I sang softly. I could faintly hear the television playing downstairs. But within a short time, that left my attention and faded out.

Gradually, my physical body fell into a light sleep and I became aware in the Soul body.

The house was now quiet. Dad had turned off the television set and gone to bed. Mother was already there. The January wind whistled a mournful tune in the barren branches of the huge old elm outside my upstairs window. Outside also, I heard the sudden sharp bark of Lady, our farm dog, apparently warning prowling dogs that this was her property, and off-limits to intruders.

Then Paul Twitchell appeared on the blank screen in my inner vision. He was seated in a comfortable easy chair, attired in the familiar sky blue shirt and slacks.

I stroked my chin, pacing the floor in front of him, all the while lost deeply in thought. Finally, I looked into his patient blue eyes and blurted, "Paul, please show me the future. Teach me the secrets of the ECK-Vidya, the Ancient Science of Prophecy."

His keen gaze regarded me calmly, then he asked, "Why is the future so important to you?"

"So I can avert trouble when I see it coming, and put myself into the path of the good things in life when they're near!"

He shut his eyes a moment, reopened them, and said, "It is very difficult to face life even when you know *only* the good things to come."

That was puzzling. I had not thought about that. To me, it was all or nothing. You see the future or you do not. Paul suggested that I could not even withstand the burden of foreseeing merely the good fortune to come my way. What a riddle!

"When you are ready," he added, "you'll see the beginning stages of the ECK-Vidya. You will start to learn the ancient science gradually, step-by-step, so as to maintain a balance in your daily affairs."

The next moment, I found myself back in my physical body that was bobbing its head up and down, just awakening from this light sleep.

Reluctantly, I threw off the warm quilt, my mind still grappling with the advice from Paul, the Inner Master. What did he mean, "...difficult...even when you know only the good things to come"?

I wondered how long yet before the ECK-Vidya, Ancient Science of Prophecy, would begin to come into my life.

13

The Game Plan

For many days I waited for something to show me the future—dream, ECK-Vidya, anything at all.

Increasingly, I had developed a little broader experience in the inner words via Soul Travel under the patient tutelage of the Living ECK Master. Some former mysteries became, if not commonplace, at least easily recognizable as a valid part of my life.

Deep within me, like a quiet pool of water in a cool forest, lay the certainty that someplace on earth moved people with the particular flair of seeing into the future chapters of their lives. If somebody else could do it, why couldn't I?

Hence my attention danced lightly around this strong yen to glimpse the future. By degrees, I developed the knack of bringing into my life something as elusive as the ECK-Vidya.

The secret was not to storm head-on toward the citadel that contained my wish. The successful way was to travel obliquely.

The head-on rush was certainly a dramatic and awe-inspiring attack upon the spiritual battlefields, but generally it abandoned me at the foot of the stronghold. Here I stood cowering, vulnerable to the sharp sticks and arrows of the soldiers hidden upon the wall above me.

All my clever machinations to overpower the forces guarding the secret future had ended in defeat. Consequently, I learned to play down this headlong urge to unravel the intricacies of the ECK-Vidya, the Ancient Science of Prophecy.

I reassessed my game plan. First, no doubt, I had to know precisely what it was that I wanted. Then it was vital to study the physical or spiritual ways open to bring to me. Finally, the approach to the wish was made obliquely, from an angle, not pushing, never rushed, willing to let Spirit, the ECK, manifest it in my life of Its own accord, when I was ready for it. All the inner preparations had to be made. And it would come, since I had made an agreement with it.

Have you ever watched a mother when her child goes out to play in the yard? She knows every instant whether the child is safe or in danger. The mother watches so unobtrusively that she hardly interrupts her household duties or even lets the child suspect its careful, moment-to-moment surveillance.

This kind of watchful striving worked for me. I did not sit idly by while awaiting the necessary unfoldment to grasp the subtleties of the ECK-Vidya. Instead, I made a lot of goals of things I wanted to see and do, both in my inner and outer lives.

It is like the writer who writes a story and vows not to type another word on paper until the publisher buys it. He could wait a long time.

Another author will turn out an article, send it to a publisher, and immediately create another one to follow the first, and so on, until a veritable flood of his manuscripts inundates the market.

Which of the two writers, do you suppose, will be first to open his mailbox to find the welcome little note: "Here's a check for the article we printed in our publication"?

Perhaps the little articles sold by the persistent author will give him the encouragement and skill to someday produce The Great American Novel.

I set a lot of little goals for myself, easy-to-reach goals, while waiting for the veil covering the ECK-Vidya to slowly pull back, revealing its hoary mysteries to the seeker. And finally, it did, at least a little.

14

The Ancient Science of Prophecy

While Paul Twitchell was still the Living ECK Master, he at first gave readings of the ECK-Vidya, the Ancient Science of Prophecy. He did this as a spiritual service to his students, but later discontinued the practice because of more urgent demands upon his time.

I was still on the farm after finishing a four-year term of military service. One day I sent away for an ECK-Vidya reading. Paul Twitchell sent no response after more than a month, and I debated whether or not to write another letter.

That same night, I awoke in the Atma Sarup, the Soul body. I found myself in an office someplace on the West Coast. A murmur of voices came from an inner office where two people were discussing a business matter too indistinct to make out.

A rather short man in light blue slacks and shirt emerged from the door of the inner office. "May I help you?" he asked politely. I recognized him immediately as Paul Twitchell, who was then the leader of Eckankar.

I explained how I had written to him for an ECK-Vidya reading over a month ago and expressed concern that the letter might have been lost in the mail.

"Let's see when we have you scheduled, Mr. Klemp," he said courteously. He opened an appointment calendar lying on the reception desk before him and quickly flipped through the pages.

"Ah, yes," he said, "you are scheduled for the last Thursday of this month."

Paul talked a moment or two longer. "My writing load has become so heavy that some of these ECK-Vidya readings are listed well down the road."

Then he excused himself and entered a private office in a secluded part of the main business office. I knew that was the inner sanctum, in a spiritual sense, where he alone entered. No one knew the responsibilities and duties that he carried out there.

* * *

When I awoke the next morning, I decided to trust this inner journey and not bother Paul Twitchell with a letter that would only further increase the demands upon his already limited time. Instead, I sat back to wait, testing the accuracy of my inner vision from the night before.

The end of the month came around. Several days beyond the date that Paul gave me for the ECK-Vidya reading, it came in the mail from the West Coast. Allowing three days for mailing, the reading was prepared by Paul Twitchell exactly to the day he had indicated during the Soul Travel meeting.

In 1972, The Illuminated Way Press published Paul Twitchell's book, *The ECK-Vidya, Ancient Science of Prophecy*. It is available to all who wish to study this most ancient system for themselves.

Admittedly, the scope of the ECK-Vidya that I got

on the inner planes about the date of my reading was no earthshaking event, but I knew that here was something truly out of the ordinary. It was worth the wait.

15

A Dream of the Future

While I waited for the veils to open that hid much of the future, I kept busy by gently focusing attention on a whole lot of fascinating things like Soul Travel, healing, the secret knowledge of dreams, and one appealing sidelight or another.

Throughout all of this, I knew that these skills were merely small chunks cut out of the whole of life. They were certainly not the goal of my spiritual striving, but becoming a Co-worker with the SUGMAD, or God, was.

The talents were simply sidelights to Eckankar, a way of Life. I could accordingly enjoy them fully when the Living ECK Master saw that they could help in my unfoldment.

Consequently, I did not regret when the time came to drop them for something new and different. It became sort of a game to pick up a skill and then let it go for another.

* * *

My dreams of the future come because there is something to learn. They do not come haphazardly.

This particular dream presaged an uncomfortable, but necessary lessson from the Inner Master.

In the dream, a crowd gathered among the gravestones of our little country churchyard. It was Memorial Day. Families huddled in small knots, spread around the cemetery lawn. I moved freely among the families that stood in quiet reverence at the memory of a loved one who had long ago shed the physical body.

But there were also others who still felt the sharp bite of a recent visit by the awesome Angel of Death. A young boy carried a small hand flag. He watched quietly while his parents gazed somberly at the little mound of dirt at their feet, apparently the grave of a child.

Most families carried themselves well during this Memorial Day on the inner planes. There were no drawn-out exhibitions of uncontrollable grief.

My ambling gait among the unyielding marble gravestones and the blowing grass soon carried me to the new part of the cemetery. Few graves were set here. But among the few, a fresh one caught my eye.

I strolled over to the small cluster of mourners wiping their eyes at the edge of the dirt still bare of grass. These were our neighbors from the next farm. Intently, I studied the faces of the relatives, vaguely wondering who had translated, or died. Not until later did I notice that the owner of the farm himself was absent.

My aunt approached from a family plot and pointed to a corner of the casket that protruded from the soil.

"Oh, my!" she said, distraught. "I'm going to get a shovel and cover it back up. If his sister sees that, she'll feel terrible."

The ground had sagged around the casket that

was underground so that the corner was exposed to view. The reason became apparent later.

This dream came in late January, and it was due to happen in everyday life a couple of months afterward. The dream's significance bypassed me, although it lodged uncomfortably in a niche of my mind—an unwelcome and nagging omen.

16

How the Dream Came True

There were winter days on the farm that offered the utmost enjoyment and serenity. Maybe I left the impression that the harsh cold provoked nothing but a long, unbroken string of misery that relented only with the first soft breath of the spring winds. That was hardly the situation.

Not every afternoon demanded making wood or loading the truck with heavy bags of oats or corn for grinding at the mill in town. Nor was every minute of the day rationed out to the almighty dollar. Questions like, "Will this half hour make a buck?" were foreign to our way of life. Perhaps if Dad had devoted himself solely to making money, we would have had more than we did.

Every year, our calendar ended up with a lot of so called "unproductive" days. These were days when we had time to stop and think, and time to be alone.

Today was just such a leisurely, unproductive day. The snow crunched crisply under the four-buckle boots as I trampled around the farm buildings. Few clouds lined the deep blue sky. The contrail of a high-flying jet split the sky with a white, ripply cloud that stretched from one horizon to the other.

Our dog, Lady, trotted up for company and a quick pat on the head. The jealous tomcat also padded up to get scratched behind his ears.

I stood by the great elm tree on the west lawn, shading my eyes and squinting at a yellow snowplow in the distance that pushed the snow far back from the road into the already overburdened ditch. The snow had fallen a week ago and the roads were already open, but yesterday's driving wind had caused drifts to creep along the blacktopped country road.

An old black-and-white Chevrolet from the early 1950s inched along behind the snowplow, moving slowly along the slick road. That was our next-door neighbor, a lady returning home from her job in town.

* * *

The sun glowed a mottled red in the west, its winter rays giving out precious little warmth. Within minutes, it would sink beneath the skyline of trees on the marsh, plunging this portion of its far-reaching kingdom into early night.

I left the lawn west of the house and pushed noisily through the crusty snow toward the south porch steps of our farmhouse.

Inside, the phone rang. I could hear its faint jangling from outside on the lawn. Mother answered, but her words were too indistinct to catch. I glanced idly to the south where the church steeple poked its tip above the faraway trees, a thin triangle pricking the wintry sky.

"What?" Dad's voice came unnaturally loud. Now he, instead of Mother, shouted a string of unintelligible words into the phone.

Simultaneously, the house door flew open and Mother emerged on the porch, grief and fear distorting her face.

"Oh, he's hurt! He's hurt! See if you can help him," she cried. She meant the elderly farmer next door.

My mind shifted from gentle reverie to desperate action. I stopped to think, "Is it faster to run or drive?" How long would it take to open the garage

I decided to run.

door and start the cold car engine? Would the car start? I decided to run.

The dog looked questioningly over her shoulder as I ran onto the road, darting carefully along the slippery tire ruts frozen in the snow. Our neighbor's farm lay several hundred yards to the southwest.

Our neighbors were both in their late fifties. He sold his dairy herd less than a year ago, and retired. She worked at an old folks' home to supplement the income. The farmer now puttered around the farm, wondering how to cope with retirement after years of rising early for chores, working on the land into the dark hours, and planting and harvesting crops.

The run seemed to last forever, like a movie projector grinding along in slow motion.

His rugged barn with purplish-red weathered boards swept past. I left the road here and followed a little path around the corner, dashing past the concrete silo to the house.

Years before, I had passed a strenuous Red Cross first-aid course in high school. Bits and pieces of that dimly remembered class drifted disjointedly into my head—splints, slings, homemade stretchers, and other emergency remedies.

A white dog with reddish-brown spots suddenly leaped at me. It had crouched almost invisibly in the snow against the side of the white porch. The dog, protecting the house, hurled against me.

"Get out of here!" I shouted in frustration.

He jumped again to block my way, and I knocked him flying with a swinging forearm to the throat. I clattered noisily up the steps to the wooden porch, shoved open the door and stepped inside.

My eyes swept the dimly-lighted dining room. A large table with expanding leaves filled much of the room, with a white lace tablecloth gracing the dark wood. An ancient Ben Franklin wood stove stood outlined against the left wall, its fire out. The room was cold. A low couch rested against the far wall beyond the end of the table. Frilly curtains dressed the window behind the couch, its tan shade half drawn.

A door on the right wall led upstairs. I knew it from the many birthday parties I had helped celebrate here with other farm families, but I had never been up there.

From somewhere above, there pounded footsteps. Wails of grief tore the building. I moved around the table toward the door that revealed a steep staircase.

"Hello!" I called.

The footsteps rushed down the steps. The woman stumbled into the room, crying.

"Oh, he's dead, he's dead!"

I jumped up the narrow stairwell two and three steps at a time. At the top of the stairs I stopped. Left or right? Then I looked right.

My breath sucked out. Through the open door of a bedroom still lighted by the remaining daylight, I saw my neighbor. Only his waist to his toes showed in the doorway. He was lying on the floor.

I moved toward the door much against my will. He lay face down on the floor, still in his white T-shirt and underpants. Quickly, I stepped over him and knelt down beside him.

"Are you OK?"

No answer. I reached for his wrist to feel for a pulse. His cold arm moved stiffly. Desperately, I pressed my thumb against the artery in his wrist.

It's throbbing," I thought hopefully, but then realized the pulsing was from my own blood pounding through my fingers from the exertion of the long run.

"She was right," I realized with a start. "He's gone."

Looking more closely at his head, I knew this was true. A slight bluish tint colored his neck and lower back. A tiny puddle of dried blood spotted the floor where his nose had broken when he fell getting out of bed.

The wailing of intense sorrow continued to

One was Paul, and the other, my neighbor.

drench the house. The screams from downstairs bounced around the walls of the room. The atmosphere sparked of electricity while I stood numbly beside the body.

* * *

How easily had I forgotten that the body is only a shell that Soul wears on the physical plane. Oh, I knew that Soul discards a worn-out body like an empty corn husk after a lifetime of use, but it is funny what a beating my "head learning" took as I looked at the empty shell that had so recently housed a Soul that I loved.

"What's it all about, Paul?" I said aloud, half-heartedly addressing Paul Twitchell, who was then the Living ECK Master.

My stomach was flying, both hands trembled, a sob stuck in my throat. I thought dimly about the promise that Paul gave in his monthly letters to his students: "I am always with you."

In his role as the Inner Master this was true, as I had discovered so often during contemplative exercises. He would appear on the inner screen of my mind to give insights into the principles of ECK, more commonly known as the Holy Spirit. But in this confusion, I had momentarily forgotten.

"Then, Paul," I said, "let me know you are here, and please help!"

How would I console the woman who now flew up and down the stairs? The strain was too great for her distraught body.

Immediately, I sensed a change in the charged atmosphere. The skin on my arms prickled. A shimmering of light began flickering in the corner near the dresser. A golden glow developed. The air vibrated faster until a distinct image stood out in the center of the golden aura. In the light, I could make out two figures, one was Paul, and the other, my neighbor. Both serenely surveyed the chaos swirling around me.

The shimmering energy stabilized around them. A sense of well-being came over me and, considering the circumstances, I found this unbelievable.

The ancient greeting of the ECK Masters filtered gently into me: "May the blessings be." These simple words brought peace to my troubled self. The glow subsided and both men disappeared with it.

The soothing presence of the Living ECK Master continued to surround me as I slowly walked down the steps to comfort my neighbor in her dark hour.

* * *

This event fulfilled the foreboding dream of death in my neighbor's family. The final touch came several months later. The dream had showed my aunt's concern about the corner of the vault surrounding the casket being exposed to view. The dirt no longer covered all of the vault underground.

The grave had to be dug in the coldest time of winter. The congregation called upon its young men to do this task as a service. I had been one of the young farmers asked to dig the grave for my neighbor.

The ground was frozen. We removed the dirt in little chunks, hammered out with picks. When the cubes and chunks of frozen earth were filled in around the casket's vault after the funeral service, they did not pack tightly. Little spaces remained around each wedge of dirt until the spring thaw settled the dirt, thereby exposing the corner of the vault. This fulfilled the dream.

I was at the cemetery the day my aunt discovered the exposed corner of the casket.

"I'm going to get a shovel and cover it back up," she told me. "If his sister sees that, she'll feel terrible." Those were the very words she had used in the dream several months earlier.

She came to our house for Sunday dinner. When I showed her my dream notebook with the account of our neighbor's translation, or death, including her own words, she was deeply mystified. She did not know what to make of it.

I knew this was a portion of the ECK-Vidya, the Ancient Science of Prophecy that Paul was teaching to me for my unfoldment. I had a lot to learn about detachment.

17

The Soul Traveler and the Ghost

The translation, or death, of our neighbor became the basis of a short story published in the 1976 *ECK Mata Journal.*

By the time I wrote the story several years later, the Living ECK Master had been responsible for a number of training sessions on the inner planes where I was allowed to go along while he helped a newly departed Soul find Its rightful place in the Far Country.

* * *

The troublesome ghost slept in the upstairs room that old Mrs. Lewis rented out to boarders. The ancient, white house itself, paint flaking from its sides, jutted three stories above the street. The lawn's tall weeds further marred its appearance as it nestled among its well-trimmed neighbors.

The growing number of roomers who stayed but a single night and fled at daybreak had indeed become appalling. And as Mrs. Lewis thought back to determine when the ghost had first come, she noted that it was not until after Walter died. Walter had occupied that upstairs room for several years after his retirement. One afternoon, she discovered him lying facedown on the floor, dead from a heart attack.

Today as the tall and spindly woman sloshed her breakfast dishes around in the sink, she wore a yellow-and-orange gingham dress, neatly ironed. Her piercing gray eyes gleamed brightly, the eyes of a woman well able to care for herself, even though retired.

This unruly ghost bothered her. How do you evict a ghost as an unsuitable tenant? In fact, she'd never even seen it. The only reports came secondhand from terrified and fleeing roomers.

The last tenant, the apprentice barber, had lasted a week—a record of sorts. True, she'd often heard angry outbursts popping from his room in the dead of the night, and heard the restless pattering of his bare feet pacing the floor until three or four in the morning, but the barber had lasted a week.

Pete Something-or-Other was the new one. Without much conversation, he had lugged his battered suitcases up the squeaking staircase and deposited them with a dull thud in the middle of the ghost's room. Glancing around at the bare, dowdy furnishings, he said curtly, "It'll do, I'll take it."

Delighted at her good fortune in landing another renter, Mrs. Lewis bustled about for a moment on her cane to show him where she stored the towels, then excused herself and hobbled downstairs.

Pete's clothes were quaint, to say the least. He removed his moss green golf cap and twirled it through the air where it plopped against the radiator; the orange-and-blue striped muffler came next. His sea-green overcoat, snow-covered from the howling storm raging outside, appeared to be salvage rescued from a farmer's twenty-year-old Sunday ensemble. Faded blue jeans completed his attire, in addition to a soiled pair of tennis shoes that he quickly unlaced and set to dry by the steam radiator. Pete was a Soul Traveler. This didn't show itself, of course, by his clothes. But his carefree gait, arms pumping briskly at his sides, hinted at a clearcut air of independence. Few envied him his outlandish clothes, but hardly anyone could miss the carefree individuality that radiated from him like a golden globe.

Pete's single bed, already made up with crisp sheets, stood underneath a window against one wall, while a battered brown dresser rested against another. Dingy, sand-grained drapes obscured the two windows. A throw rug alongside his bed provided the only relief from the floor's mid-December chill. But the room would suit him, Pete decided, pushing his plastic-rimmed glasses firmly against the bridge of his nose. Undressing quickly, he crawled wearily into the sway-bottomed bed.

The house grew quiet. Then around midnight, a distinct eerie moan upset the solitude of his room. Pete stirred uncomfortably in his sleep. Again, the low sound of someone apparently in agony. This time Pete jerked upright, instantly awake, the quilt flung back.

"Who's there?" he croaked hoarsely. Fear had dried out his voice so he could hardly speak.

"Why are you sleeping in my room?" asked a rasping whisper that filtered back through the blackness.

Pete's eyes distinguished a faint light forming at the foot of his bed. Its intensity increased, and soon, a roly-poly little man glared impatiently at him, barely an arm's length from his suddenly cold feet. Icy chills swept along Pete's spine, first up, then down. Glazed sweat had also gathered upon his brow at the first shock. But his fear vanished as quickly as it had come. "A ghost!" he exclaimed to himself in wonderment. "A bloomin' ghost lives here!"

Now, there's one thing a Soul Traveler is not afraid of, and that's a ghost. A burglar might annoy him, the house burning down might distract him, but certainly not the mere presence of a ghost. Pete knew all about ghosts, and that's why his fear had left him.

"Who are *you*?" Pete demanded, turning the tables and throwing a question back at the intruder.

"Walter," said the ghost. "I'm Walter and I live here. Why are you sleeping in my bed?"

"Don't you know that you've died?" asked Pete.

"But I don't feel any different," he protested. "It just can't be that I...that I've passed on."

"You don't belong here anymore. You should already be in your new home in one of the heavens."

Walter gawked curiously. This news seemed to surprise him considerably. "Dead?" he asked in astonishment. "You say I'm dead?" Muttering to himself, he stumbled over to sit in the room's solitary easy chair. A soft light shone from him, beaming a rosy glow throughout the room.

All during this time, the rotund ghost had continued to materialize until, finally, he appeared to be true flesh and blood, except for the glow emanating from his shimmering body. The shimmering resembled heat waves reflecting off a hot blacktop road in summer, and this effect seemed to drift him in and out of focus.

After a long silence, the apparition raised his eyes mournfully, as if he suspected the truth of his demise. "But I don't feel any different," he protested. "It just can't be that I...that I've passed on," he finished delicately. Finally, after another somber silence, Walter mused, "Maybe that's why I can walk through walls." And again, he lapsed into a determined meditation. "All right," he admitted ruefully, "so I've died. Now what?"

As said before, Pete was a Soul Traveler. That's why he could so readily comprehend the ghost's uncomfortable predicament. Soul Travel he had learned at the feet of a spiritual Adept, an Adept well-versed in the science of bilocation. With this Adept at his side, Pete journeyed nightly into the invisible worlds, using the Soul body, while his physical body slept. He Soul Traveled as naturally as an ordinary person ate or drank. The marvelous Adept had shown him life beyond the physical plane.

Thus, he had often visited the Astral Plane, the home of ghosts. Here he had viewed the secrets of death, what happened in the afterworlds when people died. He'd seen the crowded courtyard of the Recording Angel, better known as the Angel of Death, a courtyard filled with Souls awaiting judgment on their past lives.

Here also, he'd observed the mysterious flying saucers that sometimes ripped through the time-and-space dimension that separated the physical universes from the Astral, and thoroughly frightened humans at their unexpected arrival. He'd wandered along the endless halls of the Astral museum of inventions, where a prototype of every invention ever to be discovered by man stood on display. He'd toured the Astral hells of terror and seen their terrifying creatures, as well as the Astral heavens with their breathtaking cities of indescribable beauty.

The Astral Plane and its wonders enthralled him so that he wished to stay and never leave, to delve into its many secrets, to enjoy its marvels; but his teacher had urged him along. "Why stay here?" the maroon-robed ECK Master had asked. "Beyond the Astral worlds lie many more worlds, with secrets deeper and beauties much more startling. You've barely started your explorations into these endless realms of creation."

It was upon this knowledge that Pete relied when again addressing the hapless ghost. "If you wish, I'll go with you to your new home in the distant worlds. Perhaps my teacher will accompany us," he offered.

Walter nodded briefly, for he'd long since tired of a world where no one could see him unless he threw a tantrum. And all the energy that he expended just to make himself visible in order to scare away tenants left him exhausted, sometimes for days.

"Who's your teacher?" Walter asked.

"You'll meet him soon enough," Pete answered. "This Adept can travel through all the invisible worlds at will. No boundaries stop him, for he is a highly unfolded Soul. Even the powerful rulers and mighty lords of all the universes acknowledge and revere him."

Walter looked around the room that held so many memories. His alert eyes darted back and forth, missing no detail, a habit retained from his earthly life.

"All right," he said, satisfied that he'd never want to return. "Take me where I belong."

Pete crawled back under the bed covers, padded the pillow over his ears to muffle distracting street noises, then appeared to fall into a restful sleep.

Walter watched expectantly from the edge of the easy chair. The rosy glow flowing from him now began to wane. Slowly, he faded into transparency.

"Now, how'd you do that?" demanded Walter delightedly, before dissolving entirely. "You're in two places at once! You're asleep in bed but also standing by the side of your bed in a sparkling body. Is *that* Soul Travel?"

Chuckling with interest, Walter added, "And who's the bearded one? Your teacher?" Then responding to an inquiry from beyond the range of human eyes and ears, he answered, "As ready as I'll ever be. Let's go!"

The room darkened quickly as Walter faded out completely. And, soon, only Pete's body, sleeping soundly, remained behind. Walter's chuckle broke the midnight quiet once more as if from a distance. "Now doesn't this beat all? I'll bet some mighty surprised preachers pass along this road." Finally, only the steady ticking of the clock on the dresser broke the tranquility that had engulfed the darkened chamber.

The following morning at breakfast, Mrs. Lewis, wondering whether to place another ad in the Shopper's Bulletin, asked Pete as offhandedly as possible, without appearing to be nosy, "Sleep all right, young man?"

"Of course!" he responded. "Why not?" It wouldn't do to tell her that Walter had gone for good. Without a ghost to spook boarders, she might even try to raise his rent.

Pete left the house and plowed through the milky snowdrifts that had formed during the night. He pondered the ECK Master's parting question before he had returned to his sleeping body after Soul Traveling all night: "Why is it that Truth seeks out only him who is willing to give up everything, time and again, in order to learn the higher Truth?" And searching the corners of his mind, he found that he really didn't know.

18

Ghost in the Old Farmhouse

One frosty evening after milking, I said goodnight to my parents and made my way up the cold stairway to the bedroom as usual.

I no longer dreaded the cold so much, since the Spiritual Exercises of ECK were paying such handsome dividends. The Mahanta, also the Dream Master, would come to let me Soul Travel to one of the many renowned Temples of Golden Wisdom so familiar to students of ECK.

Paul Twitchell was the Mahanta, the Living ECK Master, during these times, therefore also the Dream Master. As the Dream Master, he would come nightly in the Soul body and take me into the heavenly worlds to gain experiences in the Light and Sound of ECK. This ECK is known to the Christian world as the Holy Spirit, or simply Spirit. The interesting Soul Travel adventures compensated for the chilling cold of my bedroom.

Yet, there was a discordant note beside the cold. Our old farmhouse was sometimes plagued by ghosts. I often felt uncomfortable alone upstairs. An unwelcome presence seemed to haunt the second floor.

Besides this, my parents got suspicious about my odd behavior. What healthy young man would go to bed so early? They did not understand the attraction of Soul Travel. I explored universes far more grand than the limited entertainment available in the bowling alleys and bars of nearby towns.

So they wondered, what in the name of heaven is wrong with a son who does not go out Friday or Saturday night for some good old-fashioned fun with the beer bottle and women? At least, he should watch the late show. Get a *little* something out of life. You only go around once, said the TV beer commercial.

My dear younger sister was another matter. While our parents could not get me out, they could not keep her in. So when I was *in* my bed, I traveled *out* into the spiritual worlds to the Far Country with Paul Twitchell. And while my sweet sister was *out*, she was out on the town, roaming with a crowd that was *in*. Her nightly mileage on the physical plane often equaled or surpassed mine in the invisible worlds. Yet she was happy, and so was I.

That night around midnight, a car pulled into our gravel driveway. As it skidded to a stop in front of the house, the car door slammed shut. This signaled my sister's return. Her boyfriend signaled his departure by spinning the car wheels, pelting the side of the house with gravel. He loved the delicious sound that gravel made pelting the house, the garage, the big old elm, or anyplace the rear end of the car happened to point when he jammed the gas pedal to the floor in his ecstatic departures.

These customary, jet-assisted takeoffs down our driveway soon produced an accumulation of gravel in key locations around the farm: against the house, the garage, and the elm tree. How in the name of thunder could I begrudge him those piles of stones that so nicely braced our farm against the periodic onslaught of angry tornadoes ripping across the midwest? The boyfriend and his car, alone, with no help from any construction firm, created a tornado resistant aggregate of house, garage and big elm tree.

My sister exploded through the screen door and into the house in her usual lively manner. I lay upstairs in bed, hands cupped leisurely behind my head, waiting for her to trip up the stairs for a midnight chat.

In a single, magnificent bound, I leaped out of bed for the light switch, a chain dangling from the fixture on the ceiling.

I was not as scared of the dark when she was home. She helped split the ranks of any visiting ghosts. At least half of them preferred her company. This took from me much of the burden of entertainment.

Soon, the downstairs door opened and shut noisily. "Ah, here she comes now," I thought.

Light footsteps padded up the stairs, creaked a step or two past my door, then stopped. I heard her breathing quietly in the dark, not wanting to wake me.

She wanted to exchange notes as much as I. She would describe the world of parties, and I would reciprocate with news of the worlds beyond Wisconsin.

I feigned sleep just to tease her. What I took for my sister's breathing still sounded gently from near the doorway. All was dark. Silent night.

From my even breathing, she decided that I was asleep and moved again toward her room. I chuckled and called, "Surprise, surprise! I'm awake, come on in."

I laughed some more at my feeble joke. Then, her breathing stopped entirely. O unholy night...!

"Who's there?"

My voice trembled.

"Is that you?"

By now, I had developed a low regard for her brand of humor. Was that she or a ghost?

In a single, magnificent bound, I leaped out of bed for the light switch, a chain dangling from the fixture on the ceiling. The inspiration for this magnificent leap came when I remembered, "People don't stop breathing—*ghosts* do!"

One suggestion here that may someday prove helpful to the reader is this: to outfox a ghost, try the speed of light. I used it down the stairs. My galloping descent jolted Dad awake in front of the TV. I slammed the door shut behind me and leaned against it for good measure, for insurance.

Catching my breath, I said, as casually as possible, "Did Elaine just come up?"

Dad gave me an odd look, but continued to rock steadily in the wooden rocking chair.

"No, she's still in the dining room."

He then pretended to watch TV again as I left, his head bobbing in sleep almost before I had stepped from the room. I found Elaine reading the newspaper at the dining room table.

"No, I just got home, I haven't even gone into the living room."

"If that's true," I said, "get ready for some news. There's another ghost up there!"

She folded the newspaper with disgust. Her face fell.

"Again? I'm not used to the others yet."

She listened disconsolately to my story. Goose bumps coursed freely along our spines. Neither of us wanted to go up there now.

"What now?" she ventured.

Morning was drawing closer, and with it, one tired grouch—me. I wanted plenty of sleep before tackling that barnful of high-kicking cows at milking time. Muted curses flew in the direction of the vagrant ghost lurking upstairs. There is a way to evict phantoms like this, but I only remembered it now.

"I'll ask the Dream Master's help. The ghost doesn't belong here."

I returned past Dad's rocker and opened the stairway door. He jerked awake from his ritual of pretend TV.

"You going to bed again?" he asked, puzzled about all the commotion.

I nodded and stalked up the stairs. No spirit accosted me, physically or otherwise. I stepped into the bedroom, lay down on the bed and slipped into an ECK contemplative exercise. Paul appeared on the blank screen of my inner vision. I explained about the unwelcome guest.

"Could you please help?" I asked the spiritual traveler.

"We'll see," said Paul.

A calm settled over me. The fear of the ghost left. A few minutes later, Elaine came up, too. I told her what Paul had said. She also felt the peace and contentment that pervaded the room. After a while, she went to her bedroom.

The next morning, after the usual bout with the herd of belligerent cows, I came in for breakfast. Elaine said quietly, out of earshot of Dad and Mother, "How'd you sleep?"

"Fine," I yawned, "once I got there."

"Me, too," she agreed. "Will this ghost come back?"

Would it? Thankfully, it never did. Nor did I ever learn who it was. But from then on our ghostly population diminished rapidly. I would simply call in the Dream Master, in contemplation, to please escort the earthbound apparition to its rightful place in the other worlds.

Ghosts came to out farmhouse often enough throughout the years so that the phenomenon was no stranger to some of us kids. The adults hardly ever recognized their presence.

A brilliant thought suddenly dawned on me. If only it would be so easy to get rid of that gravel-flinging boyfriend of my sister's. But wisely enough, to keep the early morning peace and enjoy my breakfast, I decided to say nothing.

19

The Face of the Master

What does a Master look like? I decided to find out. The farm work at this time of autumn was picking corn. One evening during milking, I got up courage to ask my father for the weekend off so I could fly to Los Angeles to the Third Eckankar World Wide Seminar and meet Sri Paul Twitchell, the Mahanta, the Living ECK Master. The year was 1969.

When I asked for the weekend off, my Dad was changing a milker. "Sure," he said, "you can go. Where are you going?"

When I said Los Angeles, he almost dropped the bucket of milk into the gutter. In his sixty years, he had been out of Wisconsin perhaps four or five times, and never as far as either coast. For him, Los Angeles was like a shot to the moon.

"What do you want there?"

I spoke in vague terms, since our family was stoutly religious. They were opposed to Eckankar mainly because it was not mentioned in the Bible. However, they knew little about it except that once or twice a month the mailman dropped an envelope for me into our roadside box with the Eckankar return address.

Nevertheless, I chanced destiny and made airline reservations for Los Angeles. An earthquake had, in the meantime, rattled the West Coast. The family tried to dissuade me from the trip. Yet my curiosity was stronger. What did the Living ECK Master look like in person? Was he six feet tall? What sort of people would attend the seminar?

Finally in Los Angeles, I scrutinized the three or four hundred people who had come to listen to Paul Twitchell deliver a number of talks on Eckankar. Nobody looked particularly odd. I stood quietly in a

I was not invisible, as I had supposed, but stood out like the Statue of Liberty at night, bathed in a flood of powerful lights.

hotel hallway watching people scurry along to personal destinations.

A slight commotion arose around a small group of people approaching me. In the center of them was a smallish man dressed in a light blue suit. I recognized Paul Twitchell.

My first thought was something on the order of "How come the Godman is so short?" Paul stood all of five-and-a-half feet tall. The men and women walking slowly along with him, I noticed, showed the utmost respect in his presence.

At the time, I was still embarrassed about belonging to the outer organization of Eckankar. Its teachings seemed so far out, yet so commonplace, that I constantly felt a furious struggle within myself to either embrace it or totally reject it. This inner battle raged every day.

As inconspicuously as possible, I stood where I might watch Paul without his seeing me, but he suddenly turned and came my way. I glanced around nervously to see where he might be going. There was nobody in this particular direction but me. I also noted to my great discomfort that I stood directly beneath one of those spotlights in the ceiling of the hotel lobby. I was not invisible, as I had supposed, but stood out like the Statue of Liberty at night, bathed in a flood of powerful lights.

Paul Twitchell walked directly up to me, shook my sweaty hand, and made quite an effort, it seemed, for an ECK Master, to read my name tag. After all, was he not supposed to know everything?

"Hello, Mr. Klemp," he said finally. "I'm happy you could make it."

He sounded sincere, but I wondered, "Would the real Living ECK Master even have had to read my name to know me?" But I let the suspicion go.

Paul chatted pleasantly for a moment, mentioned an appointment we had later during the seminar, and then he rejoined his group.

My hand still tingled from his electric handshake. Actually, his handshake gave more of a flow of warmth throughout my body that felt soothing and good.

"Gee, at least *he* is not so strange," I decided, gaining a trifle more confidence in the outer Master.

This was the first time I had seen Paul as the outer Master. Yet, his was the same face I had seen so often during the preceding two years on the inner planes as I faithfully practiced the Spiritual Exercises of ECK. There I knew him in the inner worlds as the Inner Master, or even, the Dream Master.

For two whole years, I had diligently followed the Spiritual Exercises of ECK. A year later, in 1970, the Illuminated Way Press published Paul Twitchell's *The Far Country.* In chapter two, "The Searchlight on Religion," Paul carefully detailed what happens when an individual himself becomes a spiritual traveler, what he sees, and where he goes.

The Spiritual Exercises of ECK involved twenty minutes of light contemplation up in my bedroom on the farm after evening chores. They assisted my unfoldment so that the Inner Master could step into my consciousness and help in Soul Travel to a number of regions beyond the physical plane.

And yet, it was also strange to see Paul Twitchell here in the International Hotel in Los Angeles. I had wondered if meeting the Living ECK Master would throw me into disillusionment if he did not measure up to my very high expectations.

Paul Twitchell was a quiet, unassuming man. He reminded me somewhat of a short Greek god. All in all, I tried to determine what power he possessed that enabled him to appear in my room almost nightly, over two thousand miles removed from California.

Seven years earlier, I would have scoffed at the idea of anyone claiming to be a spiritual traveler. That was when I was still a preministerial student. I had learned a lot about the hidden side of life since then, becoming increasingly more adept at the Ancient Science of Soul Travel.

The rest of the Eckankar seminar in Los Angeles passed mostly in a haze. While there, I had received the Second Initiation from Paul, too. This was a more direct linkup with the ECK, or Holy Spirit. It opened me to a greater flow of the divine Light and Sound of ECK.

Sunday night when my plane landed back home in Wisconsin, I wondered, "How will life be different now that I have this direct linkup with Spirit?"

I soon found out. The next day I broke my arm while cranking the tractor. I was right back in the nitty-gritty of everyday life.

20

The Mills of the Gods

Who has not heard the saying, "The mills of the gods grind slowly, but exceedingly fine"? That surely applied in my life now.

Almost a year passed to the day since I had wounded the buck during deer hunting season, breaking its right foreleg. I surely was not thinking about that, however, as I drove the tractor out into the pasture to bring the corn wagon out to the truck in the driveway.

A lot of things had happened over the weekend. I had just returned from the Third Eckankar World Wide Seminar in Los Angeles and met Paul Twitchell, the Mahanta, the Living ECK Master, of the times.

Here I was back on the farm, starting a stalled tractor. The battery was dead, and the engine would not turn over. I jumped off the seat, the crank in hand, and moved around to the front of the tractor.

I pushed the crank into the little red Farmall "A" tractor, fitted the crankshaft into the motor, and taking care to tuck my thumb flat into the palms, I pulled hard on the handle. The motor sputtered, but died.

The crank handle had stopped at the top of its cycle, an awkward angle from which to spin the crank handle again. Once more I put my hands on the handle, this time to nudge it to a more comfortable position. The gentle pressure of my hands fired the magneto, spun the crank, and broke my arm. The crank handle had struck so sharply that it lifted me several inches off the ground.

This curious understanding came to me at that painful instant: I wounded the buck in the right front leg, and now the Law of Karma requires payment with a broken right arm.

The next three hours were a series of endless pains and inconveniences. I ran to the house, holding my right arm immobile. Mother was busy in the kitchen, washing the noon dishes.

"I broke my arm," I moaned.

She threw the dish towel down on the counter and looked at the limp rag of an arm.

"Can you drive to the doctor?" she asked. She did not drive.

"I will after I drive the other wagon to Bill's where Dad is picking corn," I said. "He needs the extra wagon."

One-armed, I hitched the corn wagon to our green pickup, shifted the gear shift lefthanded, and drove to Bill's. I unhitched the wagon on the shoulder of the road alongside the cornfield and left without waiting for Dad, who was at the far end picking corn into the other wagon.

Once home again, I went into the bathroom and washed off the accumulated sweat and barn smells. Then struggling into my town clothes, I eased into the seat of our family car, a souped-up, ex-highway patrol '59 Ford.

This car was a "sleeper," Dad's pride. He enjoyed driving it in stoplight races with teenagers in their hot rods. Our car looked barely able to top sixty miles per hour, but the kids were often amazed to see it zoom off ahead of them, reaching sixty in first gear alone.

At the moment, I appreciated the speed of the car. I wished to get to the doctor's clinic, fourteen miles away, just as fast as possible.

The clinic's waiting room was filled with patients who studied me curiously as I lurched into the door. Their probing eyes tried to guess my malady, and was it worse than their own?

At the desk, the nurse assured me, "Oh, the doctor will be here shortly. He hasn't come in from the hospital yet."

I picked a seat on a couch. One delay after another. Pain—dull, throbbing pain—started to break through the numbness as the shock wore off. Idly, I riffled through an old magazine. The doctor arrived.

"Thank goodness," I sighed with relief. The arm was really starting to hurt.

At that very moment, the nurse's two-way radio crackled an urgent message throughout the waiting room: "Heart attack...can the doctor please return to the hospital right away?" A heart attack victim had just been taken to the hospital.

I consoled myself, "Would I rather have a broken arm or a heart attack?" Considering the alternative, I settled back to enjoy, if possible, my damaged arm.

Nonetheless, deep waves of pain shot through me. I felt nauseous. "Don't pass out," I told myself. The room started to swim before my eyes.

Then, a silent wave of contentment flowed over me. An inner voice spoke, "I am always with you." Of

111

course! Paul Twitchell had spoken those very words
to me last weekend in Los Angeles at the ECK Seminar.

"Paul," I whispered quietly within myself,
addressing the Inner Master, "please help!"

The strangest thing happened as I sat slouched
on the couch with my eyes shut. Someone was tugging at my broken arm! My eyes snapped open.
Nobody was even near me. In fact, the waiting room
had nearly emptied since most of the people decided
they were not sick enough today to wait indefinitely
for the doctor. Maybe they would be back tomorrow.

The tugging continued. I shut my eyes and

Paul Twitchell and Rebazar Tarzs, the great Tibetan ECK
Master, stood there beside me in the Soul bodies, setting
the fracture.

peered through the Spiritual Eye into the invisible worlds. Who was fiddling with my arm?

Paul Twitchell and Rebazar Tarzs, the great Tibetan ECK Master, stood there beside me in the Soul bodies, setting the fracture. Rebazar Tarzs was dressed in his usual attire, a knee-length maroon robe. His coal black eyes scanned the break. He grasped the arm firmly in his strong hands, and with a slight tug and a gentle twist, he set it without another jab of pain. Paul looked on. A warm sensation of love swept over me as I felt the bone slip into place.

"Thanks," I whispered inwardly.

They acknowledged my thanks with a brief nod and disappeared from sight. I reopened my physical eyes. The gentle tugging had stopped. My arm no longer throbbed with the deep ache. The beads of sweat had left my forehead, and my stomach settled down again. The fainting spell cleared away.

"Mr. Klemp?"

The nurse called from the registration desk. Carefully, I arose from the couch and approached her.

"The doctor is in now, but he says you'll have to get X-rays from the clinic in Waupaca." Waupaca, another small country town, was five miles further down the highway.

This time, however, the shifting of gears posed no problem. I was developing a real flair of shifting into second and third with my left hand, while holding the steering wheel steady with my knees.

The technicians at the Waupaca clinic took the X-rays and instructed me to return them to the doctor. The doctor carefully examined the negatives and whistled, "Boy, are you lucky! The bone is set perfectly." He could not know about the two ECK Masters, nor did I consider it wise to tell him.

As the doctor prepared the plaster cast for my forearm, a startling thought occurred to me: "If it was bad karma to break the deer's leg, how extraordinarily lucky I was not to have *killed* it."

The mills of the gods grind slowly, but exceedingly fine.

21

The Potato Story

Memories of potato planting on the farm lingered with me long after I had moved to the city.

Every spring, Dad cleaned and greased the potato planter in the machine shed. In the meantime, he set my brothers and me to work in the potato room, way back in the barn, opposite the bull pen.

In this dimly lighted room, my brothers and I huddled on milk stools, surrounded by enormous piles of potatoes. We were to cut each potato into blocky chunks for the potato planter. It took days to cut up enough seed potatoes for the twenty acres of land on the marsh.

After the blustery winter had retreated before the April showers and May flowers, neither my two brothers nor I wished to spend the balmy spring days cooped up in this potato room. But spring was here and the crops had to go into the ground, because the land was finally dry enough to hold the tractor.

Years later, I left the farm for the city. Although I dearly missed the quiet of the spacious outdoors, I hardly regretted leaving behind potato planting.

When I joined Eckankar, I soon learned about the cycles of life that underlie every daily event. Words like *karma* and *reincarnation* became commonplace. I decided that once a cycle started, it had to be finished. This was simply the nature of *karma*, also known to science as cause and effect. In the biblical writings, the ancients said, "What you sow, you must also reap."

My thoughts were far away from the potato patch once I discovered the art of Soul Travel into the heavenly worlds. Finally, I had learned the secret of spiritual freedom, no matter how stringent I might find my outer, everyday life.

What has cutting seed potatoes to do with Soul Travel? Simply this, the ECK balances out the spiritual adventures and weaves them into our daily life. Hence, we learn important lessons for our unfoldment.

The glitter of Soul Travel was everything for me. Even while still on the farm, after my boyhood, I eagerly awaited the quiet times at night when I contemplated on the Spiritual Exercises of ECK. That gave the chance to drop the cares and toils of the day and get in touch with my Inner Self. This was my Holy of Holies!

I would prepare a comfortable seat for myself on the rug beside the bed. Putting attention gently on the area between my eyebrows, I would shut my eyes and chant a secret name of God. The ancients knew this as simply "HU," like the name Hugh, but in a long, drawn out breath.

Sometimes, gentle impressions flitted across the screen of my mind, giving some delicate and unexpected insight into a long-standing spiritual dilemma. Other times, I would be so fortunate as to see a blue light. This I had learned long ago was the light coming from the Inner Master. Later, I was able to see the Inner Master himself, as the blue light flooded around him in my inner vision.

How I enjoyed these nightly meetings! The Inner Master, who was Paul Twitchell, the Living ECK Master at the time, would take me beyond the physical body in the Soul awareness. Then moments later, I would look around and find myself beside the great ECK Adept, someplace in the far outreaches of my own God Worlds.

Here a series of lessons and adventures awaited me. Each time, a little more polishing of the inner self occurred, so that I gained a truer look at the worlds beyond the touch of the physical hand.

One such night I found myself outside the physical body. Although I now lived in the city some miles from the farm, I found myself, as Soul, hovering like a soft glow of light by the woodshed on our farm.

Suddenly, there was a gentle upward tug. To my astonishment, I flew into the sky at a great speed. The farm fell away below. Soon I could see the countryside for miles around, then all of Wisconsin, with Lake Michigan many miles to the east. And still higher I flew. My view now enveloped the United States and the bordering oceans.

Where was I going? What was happening? Yet, strangely, there was no fear, only a calm sense of expectancy as this mysterious force flashed me ever faster through space.

The blackness of eternal night surrounded me totally, except for the ball of light that I was as Soul. Soon, too, I noticed a slackening of velocity of velocity. What would be the end to this fabulous journey?

Suffused light gradually filled the black space around me. All movement stopped. I looked around and found myself in one of the famed ECK Temples of Golden Wisdom. This, I surmised later, was the Moksha Temple of Golden Wisdom in the city Retz, Venus. Here was a section of the famed Holy Scriptures of ECK, the Shariyat-Ki-Sugmad, "the Way of the Eternal."

The building was dome-shaped. Light flowed in gently through some kind of glass. An ECK Satsang class was in session, conducted by a rather tall man with snow-white hair and short beard equally as white. This, then, was the great ECK Master, Rami Nuri. He was teaching people who had traveled here in their own dream states. I quietly joined the rest, sitting upon a cushion in the back of the room.

When the lesson finished, an ECK Master beckoned me to follow. "Boy," I thought, "this is really some kind of an adventure. Where are we off to now?"

The tall, lean man moved quickly from the classroom out into a corridor. From there, we entered a fabulous passenger terminal that dwarfed any of the great American airline terminals I have ever seen. A crowd of travelers moved in every which way, catching flights from one planet to another. And all the time, I thought this the greatest treat I had ever had.

I must explain how I got into the Temple of Golden Wisdom. The Living ECK Master will escort any person that he knows is ready for the wisdom of that particular temple. The Living ECK Master becomes the passkey that gets one past the guardians of the gate. Paul Twitchell was the Living ECK Master then, and he had accompanied me in Soul Travel from the Earth to its sister planet, Venus.

Paul remained in the classroom, talking with other students. He nodded at me to follow this man, who was now leading me rapidly through the vast terminal.

Often I lagged behind as this guide pushed relentlessly on through the corridors. Sometimes he would wait for me to catch up after he had disappeared up one escalator, then another. Where was he taking me?

Gradually, I noted a dimming of the lightness and spaciousness that had enveloped us. Something unpleasant seemed imminent. But what? I could not find a clue.

"Don't you finish something you start?" she asked rhetorically. "Well, you might as well get busy."

I did observe, however, that this young man in a hurry had been leading me away from the hustle and bustle of the crowds. The noise and scurrying of the air terminal lay far behind us. We seemed to be in some distant corner of this spreading complex of buildings.

My guide stopped in front of a heavy wooden door. A peasant woman in a rough working dress stood before it as if awaiting our arrival.

"Here he is," said the man who had guided me through the intricate maze of corridors. "He has something to finish."

The sinking feeling deepened within the pit of my stomach. "Come along, then," she snapped. The peasant woman opened the wooden door and disappeared down a short flight of stone steps. At the bottom shone a light. I hesitated, but she poked her head around the corner at the bottom and snapped again, "Well, hurry it up! I don't have all day!"

Reluctantly, I went down and entered a cellar room. The gruff lady, hands on her hips, stood alongside a huge pile of potatoes in the center of the floor. A squat, three-legged metal stool stood by it, a stubby paring knife on the seat.

"Don't you finish something you start?" she asked rhetorically. "Well, you might as well get busy."

My once high spirits dropped to my shoes as I gazed wearily at the awesome pile of potatoes. Here I was again, cutting seed potatoes, finishing whatever cycle remained uncompleted from the farm.

And then, thankfully, right in the middle of dicing a knobby potato, I awoke in the physical body, back on earth.

By some quirk, I still like potatoes today.

22

Invisibility and the God-Seeker

In 1970, about the time of the Fourth Eckankar World Wide Seminar in Las Vegas, I became distinctly aware of the great Tibetan ECK Master, Rebazar Tarzs, giving a group of us ECKists instruction in the art of invisibility during the Dream state. Rebazar Tarzs had perfected this ability many years ago. He is the torchbearer of Eckankar in the lower worlds. Although he looks like a man in his mid-thirties, his birth reputedly occurred around the time of Christopher Columbus. Today, Rebazar Tarzs maintains a mud-and-brick hut in the Hindu Kush mountains, high on a cliff over a roaring blue river. He assists the Living ECK Master.

During those early years, Rebazar Tarzs traveled invisibly throughout the countryside to observe and learn from people as they struggled in their sadness and also during the happy times. He developed such skill in the art of invisibility that not even the most sensitive person was able to detect his presence.

Despite the fact that he practiced this art of invisibility for some time, he never let it sidetrack him from the goal of God-Realization.

Thus I was certain that if Rebazar Tarzs could

teach one in the Dream state how to move undetected among beings on the inner planes, could I not learn the same ability here on the physical plane? Does this sound too preposterous?

Remember the saying, "As above, so below"? This simply means that if you can dream or imagine something, you can really make it happen. This is the same formula used by many inventors.

The question of possibility aside, the only other question that bothered me was "How long before I can learn it?"

My resolution to imitate the famous character of early radio, "The Shadow," strengthened when I discovered a history about Milarepa, an eleventh-century Tibetan saint and poet, a follower of ECK.

Milarepa had often dreamed of levitation. Upon awakening one day, he reasoned that if he could dream such a thing, was it not possible to duplicate the feat with his physical body?

After a time, the ancient history accounts report that he actually did achieve levitation. Periodically, he found it convenient to fly from one place to another in the rugged Tibetan countryside.

Once Milarepa went for his usual flight. As he floated over a half-plowed field below, the farmer's son, who had been guiding the oxen in front of the plow for his father, abruptly stopped and pointed to the sky.

"Oh, Father," he exclaimed in awe at the unique spectacle of Milarepa flying overhead, "how wonderful it must be to fly!"

The terror-stricken farmer covered his head with his arms and screamed, "Don't let his shadow fall on you!"

The son, perhaps more than ready for reincarnation into the scientific marvels of the twentieth century, ignored him and watched Milarepa drift out of sight over a nearby hill.

My interest was in the art of invisibility rather than levitation. However, the principle of each seemed similar. Milarepa dreamed that he achieved levitation, and he set out to do it. Therefore, if I learned invisibility during Soul Travel, would this inner skill logically transfer to my everyday, physical life?

But no matter how hard I tried, I did not disappear. Finally, I gave up the attempt, deciding wisely to leave this achievement to a more persistent and skilled person.

Now this is how Spirit works with me. When I push for something and try to bring it into my life, Spirit does not necessarily make it happen. The ECK, or Spirit, refuses to be controlled by anyone. It brings the experience to me when I am prepared inwardly for it. So I gradually gave up all thoughts of a disappearing act.

Soon afterward, I traveled to Las Vegas for the Fourth Eckankar World Wide Seminar at the Stardust Hotel. My thoughts were on the excitement of seeing Paul Twitchell again, the Living ECK Master until his translation, or death, a year later in 1971. The last thing on my mind was any kind of invisibility.

A disturbing thing happened the first night after Paul's talk. It was about ten o'clock when I walked through the lobby of the Stardust Hotel.

A peculiar sensation affected the atoms of my body. Until now, I had ever been so acutely aware of the basic building foundation of my body, the atom structure.

My body became a whirling mass of atoms. They all moved at roughly the same frequency until another person approached within several arm lengths or more. Then my atoms adjusted themselves to the new, unfamiliar speed of the other person. The new rate of vibration seemed to match the rate of the other person's atoms, just as meshed gears run smoothly in a machine.

It was a simple matter to adjust to another person's vibratory rate. When my atoms vibrated or moved at the other's frequency, the other individual mistook them for his own. Rather, he was not able to discern mine from his. Consequently, his magnetic field was not disturbed by my approach, because our magnetic fields were harmonious.

Finally, I put two and two together in this knack of invisibility. when my atom field aroused no foreign sensations in the atom field of another person because our vibrations were in agreement, then his senses were not warned to be on the lookout for a stranger nearby. Hence I was invisible to others, even though I could see them and myself perfectly well.

It is well to point out here that I did not cause my atoms to fade me from sight. The ECK, or Spirit, did that through the Living ECK Master, who was also my Inner Master. I was merely an interested bystander to this, so to speak, even though my body disappeared for other people.

I experimented to see what constituted the invisible state. Was I really hidden from the eyes of the crowd? Perhaps this was only a brilliant flight of my imagination. I decided to find out.

A young lady hurried through the lobby directly on a collision course. Did she see me? The peculiar sensation of my atoms adjusting to her vibrations occurred. She bumped right into me.

"Excuse me," she said, backing away with a startled look on her face, "I didn't see you there."

Obviously, the trick was to sidestep people and avoid any bone-jarring encounters. That would maintain the cloak of concealment.

I strode directly to the center of the lobby where the traffic was heaviest. I wanted to observe the mixture of atoms that composed the crowd. Could my atoms harmonize themselves to so many different levels of atoms?

I stepped out of the physical body into the Soul form and observed the swirling pools of atoms around my physical body. As my churning sea of atoms encountered the turbulent ocean of atoms from the crowd, a significant change took place. My atoms attuned themselves neatly on every side to blend with the particular person on that side.

Hopefully, this is clear. It seems comparatively simple to experience the harmonization of atoms that produces invisibility, but it is a lot harder to explain. It takes someone like the Living ECK Master, however, to give one these lessons.

Anyone who wishes to discover the vastness of his own God Worlds need look no further than a spiritual traveler like the Living ECK Master. He exemplifies the bold and adventuresome in spirit.

That is exactly what the God-Seeker wants in his search for the SUGMAD, God.

23

Dorothy's Miracle

Miracles are such funny things. Small ones occur every day, a couple of big ones maybe once or twice in a lifetime.

Yet, casually ask the average person about the sudden improvement to his health, money or job, and he will likely give credit to everything but a subtle miracle of Life.

Miracles of all degrees occur constantly. Nevertheless, somebody must have the journalistic skill to trace and pinpoint the details of the miracle, report them, and get the story on the six o'clock evening news. Then everybody will know and, perhaps, recognize the miracle.

Miracles are often such petite, quiet little things that most of us never recognize even those that happen to us. Here follows the story of one such event.

* * *

The proofroom of one of the largest printers in the nation bustled at shift change in the late afternoon. The day supervisor shot hurried last-minute instructions at his swing shift counterpart.

The day team of twenty-some proofreaders passed along bits of grammatical and typographical oddities to the rest of the evening team. Then followed a sudden rush to the exit. The smaller remaining crew got itself settled to tackle the night's production proofreading chores.

"Where's Dorothy?" said Linda to no one in particular. She slouched at her desk and shook the raven-black hair out of her face.

Jim, the red-faced, snow-topped supervisor threw a sharp, disapproving glance at Linda's unprofessional posture.

"She's in the hospital," he said. "Sounds like female trouble."

His scanty bit of speculation was sufficient to set loose the gossip wheels for at least a quarter of the shift, as one proofreader after another tossed out his opinion of what was really wrong with Dorothy. It passed the time.

A lone proofreader sat at his isolated desk near the window. He listened halfheartedly to the specks of conversation that drifted around the room on the rising and ebbing waves of sound. Finally, he propped his hand against his left ear to shut out some of the cackling chatter. He continued to proof page after page from the manuscripts and galley copies before him.

An idea had formed in his mind. From what he could tell, Dorothy, the absent proofreader and also close friend, had been ill for several months even though she regularly came to work. Nor had she complained in the proofroom about her troubles.

Her doctor failed to diagnose her ailment for a long time. Finally, months later, after an extensive battery of tests, he found it.

"Dorothy," he told her, "you've got kidney stones."
He arranged for an operation for the following Monday morning. Today was Wednesday.

The proofreader stopped proofing and pushed the clutter of papers to the back of the desk. Reflectively, he stroked his chin between his thumb and forefinger. Yes, he had made up his mind. Much as he disliked to think about sickness, he would visit Dorothy tomorrow before work in order to cheer her up.

The next afternoon before the swing shift, he scanned the five-and-ten store's paperback rack for a happy little gift to lift her spirits. Finally, he settled on a *Charlie Brown* book by Schultz, selected a get-well card, and hurried to the hospital.

Dorothy's family was visiting her, so he made his stay brief. She sat up in bed, surrounded by her concerned husband and their children. He gave her the gifts, asked how she felt, and left quietly.

The next Monday afternoon found him at his desk as usual. He thought about Dorothy and the kidney stone operation scheduled for today. He had visited her in the hopes that somehow it would contribute to a cure.

He scooped up the proofreading assignment from the supervisor's desk and retreated to his hideaway corner desk by the window. He centered his thoughts completely on the joy he always felt in doing a thorough job.

As usual, he covered his left ear with his hand, blocking out the chatter of gossip that would later die away as the proofreaders settled down to the evening's work. Within moments he was completely oblivious to all outside sounds as his concentration zeroed in on the ins and outs of the manuscript.

The talking in the room seemed louder, more excited than generally was the case. But he paid it no mind. A gentle voice spoke at his shoulder.

"Harold?"

No reply.

Another gentle, "Harold?"

Still no answer. The proofreader was far into the depths of proofreading.

This time, an insistent hand pulled his own away from the left ear. This was accompanied by a woman's chair-jarring shout, "ARE YOU IN THERE?"

Convulsively, the proofreader jumped up. The chair shot out backward, his pencil flipped onto the floor.

"Dorothy," he gasped, "what are you doing here?"

A gracious lady with silver hair stood by his desk. She studied the proofreader with a bemused smile, curious about his intense abilities of concentration.

"Everything's OK," she smiled. "I don't need an operation."

She leaned over to whisper confidentially into his ear, "It's not very delicate to say this, but the kidney stones passed through in the urine."

"A miracle!" he exclaimed.

"Oh, come on," she said. "What's so earthshaking about kidney stones passing in the urine?"

He now saw what it took to make a miracle. A reporter would first have to write it up with flamboyant style, highlight it in the most minute detail, then get it to the anchorman on the evening news. Only then would history earn another contribution to its galley of miracles.

He returned to work, while Dorothy proofed her manuscript with quiet jubilation. It dawned on her a little, that something extraordinary *had* happened to remove her from a painful experience in the hospital, but she was not just sure what.

24

The Ten Lepers

Unknowingly, I had broken a spiritual law in regard to Dorothy's kidney stones. An ECK Master will hardly ever interfere in another's state of consciousness without that person's express permission. I had that to learn.

Dorothy had never asked for a healing. At the time, I was curious about the healing arts and took it upon myself to visit her with just that in mind.

But that did not concern me at the moment. I was struck by the fact that she did not recognize the miraculous healing she got by the ECK, Spirit. The cure was done in such an ordinary way—the kidney stones passed with the urine—that she never realized her divine gift.

Soon thereafter, Dorothy and I relaxed on break. She shoved a stack of papers to one side of her desk and invited me to set my cup there. We frequently talked about esoteric matters. They gave a refreshing breather to the grueling production pace of proofreading.

"Remember the story of Jesus and the ten lepers?" I asked her.

"Sure," she nodded, sipping her coffee and peering curiously over her glasses. "Who doesn't?"

"You don't suppose that when Jesus healed the ten lepers it was so obvious that everybody knew he did it?"

"Of course," Dorothy retorted, "it's down in black and white!"

I shook my head. "The healing was probably so subtle that nine of the lepers never connected him with their good fortune."

"Meaning?"

"How many bothered to thank him?"

"One."

"Could it be that the other nine weren't ungrateful, but they simply didn't realize that Spirit had used Jesus as Its vehicle to heal them?"

"Well, I don't know..." Dorothy's voice trailed with misgivings about this apparent heresy.

"For instance," I continued, "one leper (now satisfyingly healed) confided to a crony, 'Dr. Ishmael's special medicinal Kick-a-poo extract kicked the leprosy right out of my hide.'

"Another leper, for another example, probably assured his delighted brother after the priests had verified his healing, 'Simple!' he announced, 'It was aspirin that did it, spelled A-S-P-I-R-I-N!'"

Dorothy chuckled, "Why, that's ridiculous!" She put her cup back into the drawer, signaling the end of break.

25

Dr. Crackin McKracklin

Just a short week later, I began to reap the consequences of interfering in Dorothy's life. Unknowingly, I had taken on her *karma* when I visited her. It probably spared her the operation. But now, I was to pay the debt incurred.

Hesitating, I breathed deeply and walked into the dentist's office. "Where've you been?" inquired my muscular dentist. "That bridge has been sitting here in my lab for a year, and you running around with that flappy partial plate." He clucked disapproval. "Well, let's get to work."

His tone and curt manner set off a warning bell that on this particular visit and those to follow, my fingers would gouge new handholds into the armrests of his ancient chair.

Actually, the dentist harbored mixed feelings. Anger and relief shone in his eyes simultaneously. He was upset, first of all, because I had waited a year to return for the completion of the dental project, but on the other hand, he was relieved that I did finally come anyway, so he could charge me for the cost of the gold in the bridge. The carefully constructed, but unfitted bridge was still unpaid for.

"Now, this won't hurt a bit," he crooned, as my head shot back from the blinding pain of the syringe stuck into my gums.

"My, some people are so sensitive," he observed.

I nodded dumbly.

Before the anesthetic could deaden the nerves, he reached for the drill. "Now, let's see here," he said, "gotta open this up a bit. HOLD STILL!"

My knuckles turned a chalk white from clutching the armrests. The anesthetic's soothing numbness finally took hold and the pain subsided. I relaxed and wiped my forehead.

"Hey, this is easy," I thought. Relief from his tortures was a pleasant thought, and I closed my eyes in peace.

The dentist whirled into action. He stuck devices into my mouth and tightened them, retreated to his lab in a little room three giant steps behind the dental chair, returned with this and that, puttered here and there.

I called him Dr. Crackin McKracklin. It seemed a fitting name, since he had pulled my teeth previously. He was a good dentist; however, he exercised a firm hand on his timid, squeamish patients. I fell into this broad category.

"Well, that's all for today," said Dr. McKracklin, wiping his massive hands on a white towel. "I put some disinfectant in there with temporary packing. Come back next week."

A week later I returned for the dreaded appointment. In the waiting room, a woman holding her jaws staggered past me on her way out. The doctor's beaming face appeared in the doorway from where she had emerged.

"Well, I see you came back," he smiled encouragingly.

I slunk toward the chair. Whenever I get a case of nerves in the face of pain—extreme pain—I find it easy to call for help from the Inner Master. The pain does not always go away, but I feel better. Paul Twitchell was still the Living ECK Master, so I threw out a frantic SOS as I edged meekly into the chair.

"Please, Paul," I whispered inwardly, "can you stop the sting of that needle?"

The good Dr. Cracken McKracklin hovered over my open mouth, one hand hidden behind his back. I guessed that was where he held the awesome spear of a syringe.

The dentist looked me over more kindly this time. "How'd your teeth feel?" he asked.

"Good," I said, all the while cringing under the threat of the expected syringe.

"We won't need an anesthetic for this," Dr. McKracklin said to my unbounded joy. "All we have to do is take out the packing and glue in the bridge."

"Oh, thanks, Paul," I said in my thoughts, gratitude overwhelming me. Tears washed my eyes. The dentist looked curiously at the drops of water splotching my cheeks, shrugged his shoulders and disappeared into the lab. I noticed that the hand behind his back had clutched nothing more deadly than a set of keys.

He returned with the bridge, placed it carefully alongside his instruments, then set to work again. Fiddling and faddling, he blew cold air on the exposed nerves to dry the inside of the teeth. Then he stuck the apparatus in place in my mouth to check the fit, pulled it out again, blasted more cold air against the shriveling nerves, and finally took his several giant steps back inside the adjoining lab.

Waves of sweat pushed down against my eyebrows. I looked around for the doctor. He was in the lab, but his back was turned. I eased forward quietly in the chair, ready to dodge out of the office like a gazelle, unmindful of the exposed nerves in my mouth. Dr. McKracklin spun around.

"Going someplace?" he asked, although not unkindly. It was undoubtedly not the first time in his long career that he had intercepted a timid patient climbing out of his chair in flight. Sometimes, I am sure, he returned from the lab only to confront a deserted office, the outer door still swinging silently on its hinges, the hollow beat of retreating footsteps pounding down the steps to the street—and freedom.

For me there was no easy way out. While the dentist loomed over me once more with his instruments, finally ready to install the bridge and cement it into

I eased forward quietly in the chair, ready to dodge out of the office like a gazelle, unmindful of the exposed nerves in my mouth. Dr. McKracklin spun around.

place, I began to wonder what I had done to deserve this mountain of negative karma.

Half of the pain that I had endured until now seemed mine, but the other half definitely seemed too great a punishment despite the massive amounts of sugar and sweets that I had used to poison my body for years, blissfully ignorant of the laws of health.

A gentle inner voice broke into my consciousness. "So, you finally figured it out? That's right, you meddled in Dorothy's illness without her permission, and the requirement is for you to pay her karma. That is the price of her healing. She had a lesson to learn from the kidney stones, but you took it away from her. You tried, but did not open yourself as a pure channel for Spirit. You wanted credit." This was my Inner Master speaking.

From that moment on, I lost all interest in participation with miracles, especially those of a psychic nature. I no longer tried to tell Spirit how to do things from the pool of my puny and insignificant wisdom.

Perhaps I could have avoided the entanglement with Dorothy's karma if my attitude had simply been, "May the blessings be," instead of, "Spirit, heal this woman."

The doctor finished. "That's all," smiled Dr. Crackin McKracklin. "A fine job if I say so myself."

Suddenly, and for the first time, he did not strike me as a terrifying Lord of Karma, one of those beings who dispenses good and negative karma.

The dentist waved a friendly hand as I stopped for a moment at the outer office door to give sincere thanks for his dental handiwork.

As I walked down the stairs, I vowed, "No more miracles. No more 'Spirit this' and 'Spirit that.'"

More than once or twice since then have I slipped in the delicate relation with Spirit, but It has a gentle way of helping replace negative habits with positive ones.

Most often, however, it is with a sharp rap across the knuckles!

26

My First Dream in Color

One day I read in the *ECK-Ynari, The Secret Knowledge of Dreams* by Paul Twitchell that most people dream in black and white, very few in color.

Since I could not remember whether or not my dreams came in color, I asked the Dream Master

The next thing I knew, the Dream Master put a bucket of red paint in my left hand, a paint brush in the other, and told me to start painting.

that night to let me dream in color.

A few moments later, it seemed, I awoke on the inner planes. A traveler's inn from the Middle Ages stood before me in the lush countryside.

Suddenly it occurred to me: "Why, everything here is in black and white. Where's the color?"

The inn was black and white as well as the grass, the nearby road, and the trees.

So I put my attention on the Dream Master and said, "Where's the color?"

The next thing I knew, the Dream Master put a bucket of red paint in my left hand, a paintbrush in the other, and told me to start painting.

The red inn is my first memory of a dream in color. The Dream Master made me color it myself.

27

The Music of ECK

The Inner Master had already suggested for some time that I pack up and move from Wisconsin to Texas. But I put it off. Two good reasons for procrastination, I thought, were my old car and flat bankroll, but once my mind was made up to go, I never regretted the decision.

It was early March. The car was appropriately stuffed with personal belongings. Snow warnings came over the radio as I headed down the highway.

Did I do right leaving Wisconsin? Was the ECK, Spirit, really guiding me into a new way of life? Would the car run? If not, where would I get the money to repair it?

The snow started to fall heavily. Slick patches of ice gleamed along the concrete under the headlights of occasional oncoming traffic. I drove with care, because the loaded car handled sluggishly.

I pulled out my battered harmonica to piece together more segments of a broken little tune that had haunted me throughout the year. "Endless Melody" seemed an appropriate name for it.

Gradually, over the months, I had reconstructed this tune from my inner feelings. From where did the melody originate? Would I ever unscramble the whole thing? It seemed unlikely.

Playing the harmonica with one hand, I steered with the other, peering intently into the white sheet of light that reflected from the car lights against the blowing sheet of snow outside. Luckily, traffic was light.

Without warning, a strange music surrounded me on all sides. The inner, stereophonic tunes were the perfect melodies of fragments that I had worked out so laboriously in bits and pieces during the past year.

At first, various melodies floated faintly along near the borderline of my consciousness, but soon, they sifted down to a single hymn I had learned as a child. The message was quite clear once I remembered the accompanying words:

When the music had first begun to play ever so sweetly as I drove into the storm, it sounded somewhere between the strains of a harmonica and an accordion.

"Now thank we all our God...
Who...led us on our way
With countless gifts of love
And still is ours today."
This gave assurance that I was right to leave for
Texas. This was a message that I could understand
from the Inner Master, the Mahanta.
At the time, I put this note into my Dream Note-
book. The notebook also served as a log for
enlightening events during the day.

*The music plays whenever I leave the city traffic
and drive the open stretches. The inner music is
ignited after I play the harmonica. The music,
itself, is soft as a whisper, and permeates my head
and sometimes seems to cover my body.*

When the music had first begun to play ever so
sweetly as I drove into the storm, it sounded somewhere between the strains of a harmonica and an
accordion. The novelty of it all made me burst into
surprised laughter.

This, I knew from reading *The Tiger's Fang* by
Paul Twitchell, was the Sound of ECK! The ECK,
Spirit, can be heard as Sound and seen as Light. He
stated:

*So I tell you that from the sacred moment when
you hear this music, you are never again alone. In
the truest sense you are enjoying the companion-
ship of God. The Supreme One is always present
with you, playing for your delight the grandest
chorus of all the universes and heavenly worlds.*

The Inner Master, the Living ECK Master, had sent
the music as a promise of love and protection.

This was the musical version of the Living ECK
Master's promise since the dawn of time: "My love
always surrounds you."

The music is both uplifting and of a healing nature, and a most enjoyable travel companion. After all, how many people can enjoy stereophonic music of such quality while on a long trip, without ever resorting to an electronic gadget?

Assuredly, for a trip that endured more than a thousand miles, the Music of ECK was a much more satisfying companion than either my squeaky harmonica, or even my own songs.

28

My Landlady's Premonition

In a suburb near Houston, I lived in a tiny garage apartment that was nothing more than just a room. My landlady, I will call her Jean, lived in the family home out front with her husband and two sons. While rooming here, I came in contact with Jean's religion and her belief in certain "signs of the Lord."

Jean got one of these signs in a dream a few weeks before I moved in. In the dream, a young man suddenly appeared at the foot of her bed. She stared closely at his face in the dim light and later realized it was mine. Another figure stepped from the shadows behind me. Although she saw my face clearly, the other's remained hidden. She accepted the lighted face as a good omen, the shaded one for ill.

The stranger in the shadows spoke, "This young man will soon come to rent a room. That will mark an important crossroad in your life." The dream ended, and Jean sat up in bed, troubled about its meaning.

A few weeks after the dream, I approached her town during an extremely violent thunderstorm. For two weeks I had been on the road in my old car, a sort of vacation between jobs. My money was running low so I decided to roost, rent a cheap room and find a job. The rain poured down in waves. My windshield wipers swished futiley back and forth during the heaviest downpours so that I was often forced to park the car along the curb.

At an all-night grocery store, I bought a city map and a newspaper. A "Room for Rent" ad caught my eye: "Cozy room air-conditioned, refrigerator. $17/wk." The price was right, but the address was not shown on my map. I dialed the number listed in the ad, using the store's pay phone.

A woman's cheerful voice gave directions from my location. I hung up, got into the car and once again confronted the black sheet of rain. It continued to fall so heavily that I could not read any street signs, even with my flashlight poking out through the half-rolled-down window.

I pulled into a gas station and parked under the

I dashed for the front door.

awning that sheltered the pumps. "Where's 131 Oak?" I called to the station attendant as he pumped a few gallons into the tank.

"Sure don't know, I'm new in town, too," he roared genially above the storm, peering at my out-of-state plates.

He let me use the station's phone, as the pay phone was out of order. The same happy voice answered and gave further directions that led to a pleasant residential area near the edge of town. The street location fell just outside the boundaries of the city, the reason I could not find it on the map.

Two cars were parked in the driveway of the green, ranch-style home with white trim. One was a white Corvette, the other an older sedan. The driving rain made it difficult to see anything else. I dashed for the front door. A gracious, middle-aged woman answered the bell. Coal black hair made a strong contrast to her pale face and brightly painted lips.

"Come out back," she said. "The room's in the garage." She led me through the living room, weaving carefully between the chairs of her husband and school-aged sons as they sat motionless in front of the television.

The garage room was humble, but warm and dry. And I could afford the rent. My savings had dwindled, so I planned to live as cheaply as possible until I found another job.

For several years now I had been an ECKist. After leaving the farm, I finished a stint as a proofreader. Then the wind of change, the forces of ECK, began to stir again. The Inner Master, the MAHANTA, said during contemplation, "Move on, it's time for something new. Go to Texas." That is how I happened to be here, far from my boyhood farm, battling the driving rain.

The room proved suitable. Jean left after showing me the air conditioner behind the curtains of the single window in the room, and the refrigerator stuck behind the folding venetian doors. This tiny space had once housed a car. Now it was walled up and fitted with a cot, a small gas heater tucked behind the entrance door, a miniature orange lounge chair and matching footstool, a bar with two tall stools, a closet, and a shower stall plus sink and toilet. There was also a rickety, round table covered with a tomato red table cloth. Two shaky chairs were pushed against it.

Later, during several weeks when I was short on money, I survived on water and raw carrots until the novelty wore off. The tiny gas heater made a suitable stove on which to cook an occasional pot of peas and carrots. I came to appreciate the cooking convenience provided by the little heater.

One Thursday night I got off work and went to the family home to pay rent. Jean was writing my rent receipt in her living room when suddenly she asked, "Did I ever tell you how I found the Lord?" Jean was a "born again" Christian. I nodded willingness to listen.

In the next room, her boys watched TV with their dad. Jean filled a coffee cup for me and placed it within easy reach on the end table next to my easy chair. She held her own cup and saucer in the lap, pausing a moment to collect her thoughts.

"The doctors found a malignant tumor," she began. "My husband wanted the doctors to operate on it, but I knew the Lord would do it without surgery."

The TV droned on in the other room. Jean sipped her coffee. "One night I went to a little church. I slipped into a chair near the rear. A woman at the front was prophesying and healing. She looked directly at me and said somebody had reason to thank the Lord God for a healing. I knew she meant me. My breast tumor was shrinking even as she spoke. Now it's completely gone."

She relaxed in the recliner, looking thoughtfully into her cup, watching little wisps of steam dissipate into the air.

"Have you been saved?" she asked gently.

Jean was much too sweet a woman for me to take offense. From that night on, her self-imposed mission became to secure my salvation. As soon as possible, I excused my self politely and returned to my room. Who wants to be somebody else's pawn of salvation? I had found my own spiritual freedom with Soul Travel, and in the Light and Sound of ECK.

I reflected upon what Jean had said about her miraculous healing. It is perplexing how easily the miracle worker gets a following. Not one in the healer's group understands the miracle, whether divine or trick, but it lends credentials to the miracle man. People flock to him in awe, hoping to get a little magic, too.

How many understand that the same outward healing performed by two different practitioners will have much different long range results? Everyone assumes that his champion's wonderwork surpasses *all* understanding.

Even the miracle worker may not know the mechanics of how his miracle works — or care — since the phenomenon gives him power over his fellows. That is often all he really wants anyway. His psychic trick passes for a healing from the true spiritual planes, and even he himself is none the wiser.

Soul Travel is an asset here. If, for instance, somebody offered to read my fortune, I would hardly roll out the rain barrel to catch every last drop of proffered wisdom. I would study the predictions, then verify them myself by Soul Traveling above the Time Track on the Causal Plane. Here one can view certain events of the past, present and future. Common sense will reject most prophecies as false, unless you choose, for some reason, to follow them out and make them come true.

My thoughts drifted uneasily back to Jean's premonition.

29

The Birthright of Soul

Jean looked forward to Thursdays and so did I. It was a day set aside to spend a few enjoyable minutes discussing the spiritual affairs of everyday life while I came over to pay weekly rent.

Eckankar intrigued Jean, yet it scared her, too. She was unnerved by somebody who claimed to Soul Travel, moving the consciousness into the invisible worlds. Frankly, she probably did not believe I could actually travel via the Soul body, nor did I try to convince her with tales of extravagant adventures.

"Everybody who wants to know the truth about Soul Travel," I told her often enough, "must do it for himself."

She timidly tried one of the Spiritual Exercises of ECK from *ECKANKAR, The Key to Secret Worlds* by Paul Twitchell. It takes a bold and adventuresome spirit, said the great Tibetan ECK Master, Rebazar Tarzs, to step out into one's own God Worlds. I could not push her where she was hesitant to go.

The attitude of the heir who is afraid to claim his inheritance is bewildering to me. It is truly the rare person who is adventuresome enough to explore his inner domain. That is all there is to each person's birthright of Soul Travel—Soul freely exploring in Its own spiritual realms.

This reminds me of what Rebazar Tarzs told Paul Twitchell in *The Far Country,* "Man is a god clothed in rags, a master of the universe, going about begging a crust of bread. He is a king, prostrated before his own servants, a prisoner, walled in by his own ignorance. He could be free. He has only to walk out of his self-constructed prison. None hold him, but himself."

Despite her initial timidity, Jean began to make short trips into the other worlds. She did not know it then, but she was soon destined to drop her physical body and live there permanently.

30

The Fleece Test

Jean was not well. I could see the sickness in her drawn, ashen face. She did not suspect the seriousness of her condition, especially the fact that her healing had only been temporary. But who was I to destroy her faith?

Late one afternoon, Jean stopped me as I pulled out of the driveway headed for work. "You're getting the Fleece Test tonight," she said. "I thought you should know." Her words seemed to carry a hidden significance, and an ominous warning.

What did she mean? I was then holding down a double shift, both swings and mids. When I hustled to bring jobs to press in good order, Jean and her friends were busy themselves, conducting a test I did not understand.

Fortunately, the Living ECK Master had thrown a shield of protection around me during the Fleece Test. I discovered this during contemplation exercises at work. After the first rush at shift change, I had settled down to the night's routine proofing chores. With my physical attention busy, I decided to gain some insight into this mysterious test by using a Spiritual Exercise of ECK.

Although I prefer the quiet of my room for contemplation, it is easy to tune in the Inner Master even in a bustling crowd, once one catches the knack. The attention goes gently upon the Spiritual Eye that is found above and between the eyebrows. When in private, I shut my eyes; in public, they stay open so as not to attract undue attention.

One focuses the inner vision gently upon a blank screen within the Spiritual Eye, then silently chants HU, an ancient name for God. It sounds like Hugh but is repeated in a long, drawn out breath either silently or aloud. Each person's Inner Master will meet with him here in the sacred and holy area of the Spiritual Eye if the seeker's intentions are pure.

The Inner Master appeared on the blank screen in the form of Paul Twitchell, then the Living ECK Master.

"Yes," he said, "The love of Spirit, the ECK, always protects you. The witchcraft of the Fleece Test cannot harm you. My love always surrounds you." Then he was gone.

All the while this inner conversation took place, I kept proofing the printing plates. An onlooker would have thought I was deeply engrossed in the work.

Scanning the printing plates before me on the proofing table, I reflected upon healings that stem from a lower, psychic nature—such as Jean's—instead of from the true spiritual realms. Psychic cures deceive. They are rarely permanent, simply because the miracle is superficial, treating only the symptom. The underlying cause remains untouched. Perhaps months or years later, another illness occurs that is really only another symptom of the original underlying cause.

The Spiritual Travelers of ECK, of course, get far above the Time Track and scan the past lives of an individual upon his request, tracing out the original problem. If Spirit then chooses to heal him, it is a total cure, because the seed root from previous lives is gone. That is a true spiritual healing.

Her fragmented psychic cure had failed Jean. The ECK Masters use a healing technique that deals directly with Soul. Operating from the Soul Plane and beyond, they adjust the vibrations in each of the lower bodies of man: the Physical; the Astral, or emotional; the Causal; the Mental; and the Etheric, or unconscious. The vibrations of all these bodies are restored to harmony. Such a cure lasts.

The pressman took the printing plates for his next pressrun, and I put the Fleece Test plaything out of mind.

Jean sat in a lawn chair under the shade trees. As usual, her face reflected an unnatural pallor.

The next afternoon before work, I strolled sleepily out to the roadside mailbox to check the mail. The double work shift meant very little rest. Jean sat in a lawn chair under the shade trees. As usual, her face reflected an unnatural pallor.

"Congratulations!" she called with forced gaiety as I shuffled past. "You passed the Fleece Test."

I sat in the chair next to hers. "What's this Fleece Test?"

She shrugged. "The terrible pain came back. The healer said an evil spirit possessed someone close to me, and that's why the tumor returned.

"Remember the dream I had before you came? The man in the shadows frightened me. I thought he was an evil spirit."

"What about the test?"

She waved her hand in an "it really doesn't matter anymore" gesture. "Three healers tried to cure me the second time and couldn't, so they suggested the Fleece Test to find out if you had the evil spirit.

"They laid a sheep's fleece on the lawn last night after you had gone to work. The fleece was to give a sign from God. If dew covered the grass this morning with the fleece still dry, that would have proved you were possessed by the evil spirit causing my pain."

"The fleece was wet?"

She nodded dully.

Thankfully, "wet grass, wet fleece" favored the innocent. "Wet grass, *dry* fleece" would have been the nightmare of Salem's witch trials all over again.

Jean remained silent. The afternoon sun was hot as usual, but the lawn trees threw a refreshing coolness around the chairs where we sat. Neighborhood kids rode by in the street, racing their bikes past the mailbox. A tiger-striped cat stared into the bushes alongside the house, wondering how to catch the sparrow twittering so enticingly in the leaves.

I understood Jean's resignation. Despite her great faith, the healing had failed. I almost wished the problem were as simple as an evil spirit in my aura. That would have been easy enough to remedy.

For myself, I was learning compassion through Jean's plight, but without accepting her personal karma. This delicate balance is one phase of walking "The Razor's Edge."

Even as I had passed the Fleece Test, Jean failed it. Her trust in the unstable healing power of her psychic friends had ended.

31

The Law of Non-Interference

Houston is a sprawling city linked by long freeways. Since I had moved to one of its suburbs, I commuted regularly to work.

I got into the habit of stopping for fruit and vegetable juice at a health food store near the company that employed me. The owner was a kindly woman in her seventies. Our daily chats were a bright spot in an otherwise hard and relentless work schedule.

One day a thin, rather attractive woman in her forties sat talking with Helen, the owner. It was easy to overhear the conversation, since both sat at the other end of the small juice bar.

They pored over a newspaper article spread out on the counter. From what I gathered, the slender woman, Grace, had recently weighed more than two hundred pounds. The article told about her successful battle of the bulge. She had recaptured her youthful figure on a liquid diet and chose today to come off her long fast.

I listened intently, then joined the conversation. "You've got to be careful how to come off a fast like that," I cautioned her.

161

Nobody had asked my advice, but nevertheless, I delivered a lecture on the proper way to break a long fast without injury. Upon completion of my speech, they thanked me politely with thin smiles.

Grace had done all the hard work, mustering all her know-how and self-discipline to beat the fat. When the rough part was over, here comes a smarty to tell her the easy part, how to eat again. She did not need that.

I had violated Grace's psychic space. By commenting on the diet without permission, I earned a quick penalty in this chapter of life. The mill wheels of cause and effect began to grind, because this broke the spiritual law of non-interference.

Even the Living ECK Master, does not enter into somebody's personal affairs without definite permission. The spiritual law forbids it.

A week later, I started to reap the consequences of my intrusion. My pants got uncomfortably tight

I could just barely hitch the trousers around my protruding stomach.

around the middle. Two weeks later left no doubt, my appetite had blossomed out of control. I could just barely hitch the trousers around my protruding stomach.

I now ate three giant meals a day, plus snacks to tide me over in between. I became frightened. Never before had I so completely lost control over food. What was wrong?

Wearily, I crawled into bed one morning after an exhausting double night shift. I asked the Inner Master to fit this disturbing puzzle. Why was I suddenly so ravenously hungry?

In the ensuing dream, I saw Grace with several astral entities hovering around her. These disembodied spirits appeased their gluttony through Grace's zest for rich foods. But under the care of a good medical doctor, she had undertaken the fast that broke their stranglehold. Still, they fluttered frantically about, desperately afraid to lose their meal ticket. They hoped she would again succumb to her previous eating habits.

This is when I bumbled onto the scene. Discussing her diet without invitation, I opened my emotional body to the invasion of the entities. Delighted, the spirits immediately clambered aboard my wagon, preparing themselves for a prolonged, vicarious junket. They were the villains responsible for my runaway hunger.

Fortunately, they had been with me a comparatively short time before I discovered them. They had no time to set their claws into my emotional body. Like Grace, to break their hold, I fasted, drinking only fruit juice.

Slowly they let go. After a week, the last of them had released its grip. My appetite returned to normal, and my weight plummeted dramatically. After a month, my body gradually diminished to regular size.

Through this lesson, I became more sensitive to the sanctity of another's psychic space, and the subtle, pervasive Law of Non-Interference.

32

The Ouija Board

The hostess pulled out a Ouija board at a party she gave in her home. One of the men leaned over and whispered to me, "She gets good results."

The hostess set the board on a small table and pulled her chair to one side of it. Then she pointed to the empty chair opposite her and asked me to assist

She determined that the problem was my fault and another guest replaced me.

her experiment to contact the entities that foretold the future.

"Put your hands on the table," she instructed. The party crowd gathered around with bated breath. We both sat still while she asked the questions. The pointer seemed stuck.

"Strange," she scowled, "I wonder what's the matter with it. It *always* works."

She determined that the problem was my fault and another guest replaced me. Hopefully, he would prove to be a better conductor. The evening wore on. The Ouija board and the hostess prophesied for everyone, and eventually got around to me.

"You will marry before the year is out."

"Your wife will come from the midwest."

"You will have no children."

After the party, I went home and wrote the predictions down into my dream journal. I did not believe them, but suspected that later the lady would use any true prophecies to bolster her reputation, but conveniently ignore the rest.

That same year I married. Before the wedding, I recalled the prediction that I would marry within the year, and seriously considered postponing the ceremony. If I went ahead, she would be right. If I held off, it would only have been to spite her. She had me coming or going—so I married.

And sure enough, a little more than a year later, a mutual friend wrote how the would-be seeress was telling her circle of followers that her prophecy about my marriage had come true. She neglected to mention the other two that failed.

My return letter acknowledged her one correct prophecy, but also brought up the two incorrect ones. To verify my claim, I copied the prophecies out of my

dream book that furnished a better record than
either of our memories. My wife came from the west,
not the midwest. Our baby daughter belied the child-
less marriage.

The Ouija board operator's score was only a third
right. I much preferred the ECK-Vidya, the Ancient
Science of Prophecy. Either that, or flip a coin. I go
with the odds.

33

Paul Twitchell's Translation

Paul Twitchell translated, died, while I worked in a Houston printing company. Months earlier already, the ECK, Spirit, was arranging things so that I would be in Dallas then to hear the news directly from the Area Mahdis, before the official announcement a few days later by the Eckankar International Office.

Just four months prior to Paul's translation, I began work at the printing company. Even then, plans were being put into motion on the inner planes so that I would be in Dallas on September 17, 1971, the day Paul chose to go. The drawing card in Dallas was a gigantic printing exposition.

Being a new employee at the printing company, I struggled to learn all the intricate procedures. One evening when I reported to work, Tom, my boss, called me into his office.

"How would you like to go with me to a big shindig up in Dallas this fall?" he asked, propping his feet on the desk.

Tom was certainly not a half-hearted, foot-propper-on-the-desk kind of individual. He did little that was mediocre. Pushing and bullying, he

succeeded in squeezing ever-larger weekly production totals from the pressmen.

It had been Tom's brilliant idea to provide a case
of beer as a prize to whatever press crew topped
150,000 copies per shift.

The power that the reward carried was astound-
ing. The Lead Pressman took firm control of his
crew, like the commander of a PT boat in wartime.
They would get the beer, or somebody's head would
roll. "Move!" sang the Lead Pressman. "Get the
paper rolls to the stands. We've got a roll change
coming up."

A press helper wheeled up on a little tractor
equipped with a big pincer nose. The pincers gripped
a huge roll of paper that the driver set upon a
backup stand. Then he carted up another roll and
put it on the other auxiliary roll stand, both now
ready to string through the press when the first two
rolls ran empty. Expectedly, the press crew collected
its case of beer at the end of the shift and carried it
outside to the parking lot. They savored their reward
before wending an uncertain way homeward.

The spirit of the prize was catching. The beer
party created a substantial incentive for the reliev-
ing crew to win a case of beer, too. Shortly, the crews
all had perfected their techniques so much that
somebody won the prize several times a week. That
forced Tom to raise the quota to 160,000. He could
hardly afford to buy all that beer. As a result, the
printer's morale, and likewise the production totals,
dipped well below previous levels.

In the meantime, I did not particularly relish
Tom's plans for both of us to drive to Dallas in mid-
September. Our life-styles were too different. He
was married, but wanted to attend the printing

exposition as a good excuse to get away from his wife and enjoy some good old-fashioned convention fun. On the other hand, I was single, but preferred to oogle the thousands of different pieces of printing equipment.

I had resigned myself to an uncomfortable trip, for Tom would insist that I join his merrymaking. Yet, the Inner Master assured me in contemplation, "Don't worry, everything will be fine."

Two weeks before the exposition, Tom called me into his office again. His feet were on the floor, and his face bore the look of a little boy whose mommy had promised him a cookie but changed her mind.

"Something's come up," he muttered. "You'll have to go to Dallas alone."

I was delighted. From his doleful look, I suspected that his dear, but slightly jealous wife had changed his plans herself.

This, then, was the weekend Paul Twitchell, the Living ECK Master, was to speak at an ECK seminar in Ohio. This was also when he had chosen to leave his physical body. Nobody else knew that, of course.

Several times on the way to Dallas, my car drifted erratically from lane to lane as I struggled to stay awake. Last night's usual fifteen-hour shift had left me dead tired. Several times I catnapped at a rest stop before completing the 200 mile drive. The fatigue made me absolutely useless to my company when I finally arrived at the exposition.

In the exposition hall, a cheerful young lady was passing out yellow "Smile" buttons. She gasped at my gaunt face and bloodshot eyes. "For heaven's sake," she said, "why don't you smile?"

"I will once my eyes open," I replied. "Do I really look that awful?" She nodded. So I left the hall, signed into a motel—not the one provided by my company—and fell into a dreamless sleep.

This hotel was closer than the one provided by my company. The next morning I realized happily that I was thus in Dallas on my own, having paid all my own expenses.

I like a bit of freedom, to keep my own integrity, so that nobody owns me but myself. Thus I felt free to leave the exposition and visit ECKists in Dallas.

When I arrived at the home of the Area Mahdis, she told me disturbing news. "Oh," she said, "somebody called from Ohio. Paul has translated!"

For some reason, I had felt until now that Paul would retain his physical body for many more years, like the great Tibetan ECK Master, Rebazar Tarzs, who is reputedly over 500 years old. Just this suddenly, however, Paul was gone.

"Then who is the new Living ECK Master?" I asked.

"I don't know," she said. "What should I tell the Dallas ECKists?"

"Wait until you hear from the Eckankar office," I suggested.

The weekend was over for me. I could plainly see now that the importance of the trip was hardly the printing exposition, but learning about Paul's translation was the prime reason for it. I decided to return to Houston and say nothing to the ECKists there until the official news came from Eckankar. This might be nothing more than a harmful rumor.

I left the printing exhibition early, took only a few brochures of printing equipment and also several pretty calendars.

The Fifth Eckankar World Wide Seminar in Las Vegas was just a little over a month away. The spiritual worlds stood looking at fresh new horizons. A Living ECK Master had gone, yet another would step in to continue the longest unbroken line of spiritual adepts ever known to man.

What would happen to Eckankar without Paul Twitchell, its modern day founder? Would the ECK Masters of the Vairagi put another Living ECK Master at the helm? How would the change affect my inner life, the Dream state and Soul Travel? How powerful were these agents of the SUGMAD? I was soon to find out.

* * *

When I came to work Monday, Tom asked what I had learned in Dallas.

Proudly, I showed him the calendars and the small stack of equipment brochures. Scanning the brochures, Tom crumpled them up along with the lovely calendars, mashing them into the wastebasket. Still miffed at his curtailed trip, he was trying to tell me there was nothing of importance I had done for the company over the weekend.

Of course, the expenses had all been my own. Nor had Tom asked me to research any special equipment. The Dallas printing exposition was the way the ECK used to bring me to town to learn about something much more significant than printing equipment. Is it every day that a spiritual giant leaves the earth?

That little pearl of insight I kept from Tom, or I might also have found myself in the wastebasket along with the brochures and calendars.

The calendars were pretty, however. I had wisely taken the precaution to bring home an extra set.

Thus Tom's irritation proved no great inconvenience. On my wall at home, safe from Tom's wrath and spite, hung the other set of pretty calendars. As my father used to say, "I wasn't born yesterday."

34

A 2,000 Year Old Dilemma

October 22, 1971, and the Passing of the Rod of ECK Mastership from Paul Twitchell to his unknown successor drew ever closer. A month had passed, almost to the day, since the Area Mahdis for Texas told me that Paul's translation had occurred.

My Houston printing employer had reluctantly agreed to let me off work to fly to Las Vegas and the Flamingo Hotel, site of the Fifth Eckankar World Wide Seminar. Paul had billed this particular seminar as "Consciousness Five," and I was as curious as anyone what great spiritual leap would occur in the movement of Eckankar.

There was just enough cash in my savings account to make the trip. I had planned my money carefully. All preparations seemed complete.

Then the persistent phone's ringing roused me from bed early Sunday morning, the weekend before the seminar. My sister, calling long distance from Wisconsin, said that Dad had just died in his sleep a few minutes ago.

Here was a sad dilemma. Dad, as well as most of the family, had felt great opposition to my decision to leave the country church and follow Eckankar.

Even as my sister described his translation and the various reactions of the rest of the family members, an old biblical story crossed my mind. This was the story of the young man who told Jesus he wished to follow him if only he could first bury his father. Jesus simply told him, "Let the dead bury the dead."

I had no intentions of being a martyr. There was, however, only enough money either to meet the new Living ECK Master, or to return to Wisconsin for the funeral.

At that moment, I wondered what thoughts must have gone through the young fellow's head. If he followed Jesus, the gates of heaven would undoubtedly have opened for him. But what would the neighbors say?

Remember, Jesus did not have much of a reputation as a world savior as he walked the Earth in those ancient days. That renown would come later.

St. Paul had not yet hit the road to "sell" Christ to the small region of the then-known world. Nor was there a powerful church organization with money and influence which the young man could fall back upon if somebody asked the awkward question, "What good can come out of Nazareth?" The young man was on his own, to make a difficult decision in the spiritual crossroads of life.

"How few of today's pious Christians," I wondered, "would have followed Jesus, and how many would have buried their fathers?"

Nevertheless, the two-thousand-year-old decision was now mine. Not too many people had even heard of Paul Twitchell or Eckankar. Fewer yet cared that he left the body. Some, in fact, were glad. They felt that his departure would bring a quick end to that nonsense called Eckankar.

How do you explain a modern-day Godman to your family? I am sure it was no easy matter twenty centuries ago for the young man. He found it easier to bend to the social pressure from his neighbors and bury his father than to follow Jesus. After all, what are a few days in the existence of Soul? Sometimes, unfortunately, more than one could fathom.

"I'm not coming home," I told my sister. "I'm flying to the Eckankar seminar to meet Paul's successor, the new Living ECK Master."

"I know," she said, and she did understand. She has since turned her own spiritual affairs over to the guidance of the Living ECK Master, too.

My father's funeral would be on Wednesday in Wisconsin. Thursday, I would leave for Las Vegas. There was only enough money in my bank account for one or the other, not both.

All my life I had been too concerned with the silent fear, "What will people say?" Finally, I was having to face this fallacy squarely. What real difference should my decision make to busybodies and gossips?

The first responsibility was to the ECK center inside me and the SUGMAD, God. Could anyone in the physical world do much more than bear me in pregnancy or carry me away in a coffin? The interval between the first to last breath comprised my own experiences, just as it had in all my previous lifetimes.

But I felt the Spirit of ECK flow through me. I instinctively knew all would be well and looked forward to Consciousness Five with a joyous and grateful heart.

177

35

Consciousness Five

So who was the Living ECK Master during the month after Paul Twitchell left his body and his successor took on the Mantle of ECK Mastership?

On October 8, 1971, my dream notebook records a visit by the great Tibetan ECK Master, Rebazar Tarzs. I was itching to ask, "Who's the Mahanta, the Living ECK Master, now?" Rebazar kept me too occupied with several other matters about Eckankar. He left again in the Soul body before I remembered the vital question.

Several weeks later I was in Las Vegas for the Fifth Eckankar World Wide Seminar that Paul had called "Consciousness Five." This meant the high awareness from the Fifth Plane, far beyond the realms of the Cosmic Consciousness, Buddha Consciousness, and the Christ Consciousness of the orthodox religions. This seminar promised an upliftment for the entire movement of Eckankar.

I walked along a Las Vegas side street about half an hour before the evening seminar session when the new Living ECK Master was to be announced in the Flamingo hotel.

At that moment, a marvelous spectacle in the

evening sky caught my eye. A dazzling shower of brilliant light bathed the western sky. It washed the heavens with a breathtaking, sparkling spray.

The spray of light trailed from a brilliant star rising from just above the horizon. Slowly the star-like object climbed to its apex high above the earth, spewing out the swath of light particles behind it, a celestial memory of the passing star's flight.

The stunningly beautiful star rose higher and higher until it seemed impossible to go any higher. My mind recalled the words from "The Trembling of a Star" from Paul Twitchell's *Stranger by the River*.

I knew that this star in the heavens marked the new Living ECK Master who would be announced within minutes at the Flamingo Hotel.

The star faded out, but a twinkling pathway of light remained behind to witness its passage.

The stunningly beautiful star rose higher and higher until it seemed impossible to go any higher.

I hurried along to the hotel, unwilling to be late for one of the most significant events of the twentieth century. Quickly, I walked through the casino where the center of everyone's attention gravitated to the roll of the dice and the turn of the wheel.

Moving along the corridor, I entered the large auditorium. Hundreds of people were already seated. They also knew the importance of the moment for the individual concerned about his own Self-Realization and God-Realization.

Before I had entered the auditorium, I noticed an information bulletin board out in the hall. On a sheet of paper tacked to the board was a list of ECK Higher Initiates slated for the next initiation. The name of Darwin Gross had been crossed off. Why?

The other thing I noticed was a man preparing to enter the auditorium to hear the announcement of who was the new Living ECK Master. He carefully straightened his tie while his wife brushed lint from his suit coat. She readjusted his tie to make sure it was just right. The two were prepared for any unexpected honor. Would the husband be the next Master? The man, however, was not to be the next Master.

Here are notes from my book of dreams and spiritual events: "All day long we eagerly awaited the announcement of who would be the present Living ECK Master. Tonight (Friday, October 22), Gail Twitchell, Paul's widow, read one of Paul's poems, then she presented the Living ECK Master, Darwin Gross."

As I remember, Darwin was seated in the audience to the left side of the stage, several rows back. When Gail announced his name, he stood up and made his way out to the aisle, then quickly walked up to the stage.

At this point, someone in the audience stood up and shouted above the applause, "I knew it!" The audience applauded the new leader of Eckankar.

The notebook continues: "Darwin was dressed in sky blue shirt and trousers. He removed a Navy blue blazer before sitting on a swivel chair to begin his address."

There are, of course, many details not in the notes. For instance, when Gail Twitchell presented a blue carnation to him as he came on stage, every camera and tape recorder in the building ceased to function for that brief interval. There is no record of that moment other than verbal and written ones like my own.

Outside the auditorium in the casino, gamblers' hopes continued to rise and fall with the turn of a card, the roll of dice, and the spinning wheel. For many people, October 22, 1971, held no special significance. But for many ECKists, they watched the new Living ECK Master of the age step out of the obscurity of the crowd into the swirling pace of the 20th century.

Darwin Gross was now the caretaker of the spiritual works of ECK, so that all who felt ready to study the unique ways of Spirit could do so.

I returned to my room and reread "The Trembling of a Star" with new understanding. For tonight marked the beginning of a new chapter in my own life.

Editorial note: In 1981, Sri Harold Klemp became the Living ECK Master in a similar ceremony.

36

Changes

One night, before the Eckankar Fifth World Wide Seminar, it came time to say goodbye to Paul Twitchell as the Inner Master. In the Soul body, I became aware of this farewell on the other planes. My notebook for September 29, 1971, a Wednesday, reads: "Paul and Gail walked through a busy air terminal along with a swarm of other people....

"Paul put out his hand and we embraced. Then with a warm smile, he asked, 'Well, did you learn anything through all of this?' A moment later, they vanished into the crowd."

What changes did the new Living ECK Master bring into my life? For one thing, the Soul Travel excursions into the other worlds continued without interruption. Only I now traveled with the new Living ECK Master instead of Paul.

Paul Twitchell had permanently left the physical world in order to take on new duties and responsibilities on the spiritual planes as a Co-worker with SUGMAD, God.

Paul's role to me had been as the teacher of an apprentice. There was everything to learn about

Soul Travel. The inner adventures during the night added a zest to the day-to-day waking hours.

But the Living ECK Master always takes this a step further. He shows the ECKist the point where Soul Travel is no longer needed, guiding him to the Soul Plane. Here, the limits of matter, energy, space, and time are left behind in the lower worlds. He takes him beyond them to the pure spiritual worlds of *seeing, knowing* and *being*, far beyond the celestial delights known to any orthodox religion.

Paul will show up once in a while even today, but I know the ECKist's face must always be turned to the present Living ECK Master, if he wants to expand his expeditions into the Far Country. There one may gain divine wisdom, understanding, and the Realization of God.

After all, what is it all about?

37

The Blue, Silk Handkerchief

After Darwin Gross had accepted the Rod of the ECK Power, becoming the leader of Eckankar, a number of chelas remarked how much, at times, he resembled Paul Twitchell, his predecessor. The real situation was that both were infused with the Mahanta Consciousness, giving them the same look.

Paul helped me quickly adjust to learning the inner communication between Master and chela, the spiritual student. At the Eckankar World Wide Seminar in Las Vegas in 1970, I listened to one of Paul's lectures in a large showroom at the Stardust Hotel. We were all seated at tables that were angled so that the people seated on both sides could see the stage at the front of the gigantic room.

There was a magnetic quality about Paul when he entered a room. Feeling something, I turned my head to one of the side aisles and saw Paul walking down it toward the front. He moved slowly, here and there greeting a friend.

When Paul went on stage and gave a talk, the ECK-Vidya suddenly opened for me as I sat listening to him in the audience. He showed me, on the inner, certain things that would be my lot in the coming months. The ECK-Vidya, the Ancient Science of Prophecy, came in loud and clear.

With the lecture over, Paul left the showroom by the same aisle. People pressed in to shake his hand. This meeting between the Master and student is known as the *Darshan* in the works of ECK. It is a beneficial part in one's spiritual life that gives a boost, enabling him to Soul Travel with the ECK Master on the inner planes.

The revelations of the ECK-Vidya so moved me that I wished to personally thank Paul. Struggling through the crowd, I followed it out into the lobby.

There stood Paul, surrounded by a throng vying to shake his hand. I moved in closer until next in line. Paul was talking to a little, white-haired lady ahead of me. The crowd had fallen back, and the three of us stood alone in the middle of the floor.

I was terribly shy in those days and tried desperately to keep away from attention of any sort. Debating whether to stay and wait my turn or slip off into the comforting anonymity of the mass of people gathered around Paul, I finally chose to stay.

As Paul continued to talk with the woman, I noticed for the first time the blue, silk handkerchief in his hands. He toyed with the light blue cloth, running it through his hands in a graceful kind of motion, meanwhile giving me a sharp, piercing look. The spiritual understanding opened again, and I understood that the inner communication with the ECK Master was the place to look for spiritual growth, rather than only to the outer meetings.

Somehow, Paul had conveyed all that with the blue silk handkerchief and his keen, piercing gaze. I backed out of the circle of light and slipped off through the crowd. From then on, I hardly felt such an urgency to meet physically with the Living ECK Master when he appeared in public. His job was to teach me how to contact the Mahanta, the Inner Master. This contact had been made in our first meeting a long time ago, but I never realized it until now.

This was the lesson of the blue, silk handkerchief.

38

Growing Pains

The biggest change to come into my life after the death of Paul Twitchell was that now I began to help more with spreading the teachings of ECK. Prior to this, I had been content to be one of the crowd, simply soaking up all the love from the ECK and giving very little in return. Still, I had wanted to help, but did not know how.

At the Eckankar Youth Conference in Tucson, Arizona, in 1974, the opportunity came to give a talk as well as accompany Darwin through the crowds. The prospect of the talk in front of so many people frightened me, but the idea of being a buffer for him through the crowds with my skinny body was highly amusing. But who was I to argue?

One of the scheduled speakers at the Youth Conference had canceled out. The program director heard of a talk I had recently given in Newport Beach, California, about the Temples of Golden Wisdom. That was a topic of interest to an audience, so he asked me to be on the seminar program in Tucson. Until then, I had given introductory talks only at small gatherings in Nevada and California.

189

The invitation petrified me. The small audiences I had addressed up until now had made my knees knock from fright. Would several thousand people turn me into a bowl of jelly? Besides, the time slot for this lecture was twice as long as my last one at Newport Beach. So I researched the ECK books further, uncovering more stories and examples from the lives of the great ECK Masters who guarded the Wisdom Temples.

My address was slated for Friday afternoon, and this suited me well. Most of the people would be arriving in the evening—after my talk—to hear Darwin.

I went to the auditorium early to feel it out. The auditorium was huge, seating several thousand, and I came away trembling. My mind cringed at the thought, "What if I get on stage and forget everything?"

Safely hidden behind the curtain, I started to drink water. My throat was suddenly so remarkably dry.

An hour before my slot, I arrived backstage. Patti Simpson, a longtime ECKist with a zany sense of humor, was the afternoon MC. She bustled about, making sure each musician and speaker was ready to perform on cue.

Safely hidden behind the curtain, I started to drink water. My throat was suddenly so remarkably dry. After washing down a couple of pitcherfuls, I went to the bathroom. Just before my turn to go on, the union electrician left for dinner. He thoughtfully turned off the sound system before he left.

Patti explained the problem of the dead microphone. She said they were trying to find the union electrician and get the sound back on before my talk. "In case we don't," she said, "how loud can you *shout?*" I was hardly in a mood for humor.

When the dreaded time came, Patti introduced me and I walked out on stage, very careful not to trip. The stool looked inviting, and I sank down on it with relief, not trusting my shaking knees to hold me up.

The crowd proved tiny. The auditorium held seats for several thousand, but only a hundred or so people sat scattered in the front rows, and that calmed my nerves considerably. I would not have to shout quite so loud.

Just then a technician ran out of the wings with a microphone and set it up in front of the stool. "We just found the electrician," he whispered, adjusting the microphone to my height. "You won't have to shout." A spark of humor glinted in his eye before he disappeared into the wings again.

The talk went well enough. The audience stayed awake. Fewer left than came. Those are the things a speaker sees while he is juggling his thoughts and words, trying to be an open vehicle for the ECK. At least, I did. With the talk completed, I retreated from the stool as gracefully as possible, being careful not to trip over a cord and spoil an otherwise successful address by sprawling on the stage.

With the talk done, a heavy burden had lifted from my shoulders. "The rest will be easy," I thought. The other half of the assignment was to help escort Darwin through the crowds.

That responsibility, nevertheless, started to weigh heavily after the evening talk. Although somebody had asked me to be one of the escorts, nobody seemed to be in charge to tell me where to be and what to do.

Darwin finished his talk and descended into the crowd to shake hands. He appeared very tired, and people were crushing in on him from all sides. Tom, another longtime ECKist, walked with him. I wiggled through the people and tapped Tom on the arm. "I'm to help escort. All right if I tag along?" I felt it important to ask permission. He nodded.

Tom and two or three others flanked Darwin's sides and spearheaded a path toward the exit. I took up a position behind and considered how much more fitting it would be had I reincarnated as a bulky football player, since my body seemed much too small for the job.

From the vantage point of walking behind, I saw for the first time the tremendous love that passes between a master and a chela. No longer was my attention on standing off a mob, as I had supposed would be the case. I was an observer of Souls that had traveled countless lifetimes to this Tucson seminar and had met the Living ECK Master again.

The escort job was hardly all roses, however. One little lady was determined to meet Darwin. She kept throwing herself resolutely at the front ranks of the crowd around him until only I stood in her way. This did not deter her, but merely slowed her momentum. She practically rode my back out through the exit. The crowd dwindled as we got further from the hall. But the little lady followed our train in relentless pursuit. She deserted the rear guard where I had kept the fortification intact, and quickly sprinted around to the front.

Darwin stopped to greet her. I stood back, watching the meeting of another Soul with the Wayshower. "Well, she earned it," I decided, straightening my coat that had become rumpled during her repeated assaults.

My earlier tensions left. The talk about the Wisdom Temples was already history, and the first escort proved far less fearsome than I had imagined. The others would be the same.

Upon reflection, I realized that a funny little switch had taken place. While I thought I protected Darwin, the ECK was really protecting me. I enjoyed the rest of the seminar immensely.

39

The Ice Cream Story

A man in our office was leaving and his friends decided to treat him to ice cream on the afternoon break. Richard did not know about the surprise party. All of a sudden, he started to laugh. He called over to me, "Take life as you find it."

Richard explained, "There's going to be ice cream at three. I just got the feeling. It's never wrong."

The phone buzzed while we talked. When Richard hung up, he laughed again and said, "Somebody just asked me what flavor?"

He further explained that he had learned to trust his inner senses for years already. By this, he meant the communication with the Inner Master.

Another time, he decided to call home after he had been gone for five years. When his mother answered, she was excited.

"Guess what I just did?"

"You dyed your hair blond," he answered nonchalantly. He was right, of course.

On still another occasion when he called home, his mother got a similar jolt. "I bet you don't know what I just got," she said proudly.

"New teeth!"

Right again, much to her dismay. Her dentist had just fitted her with a new set of dentures.

"Oh," she pouted, "I just can't keep anything from you."

A descriptive title to Eckankar is "A Way of Life." The other day a psychologist asked several ECKists how they had discovered Eckankar. What he really wanted to know was what need did it fulfill? Recognition? A sense of belonging?

All three conceded that there had been a vacuum in their lives before they joined Eckankar. One of them was forced to be away from home throughout much of his youth, and found himself homesick. When he got into service and the military assigned him overseas for two years, he was more than ready to try Soul Travel in order to be with his loved ones.

Another of the ECKists said she had felt a deep yearning inside her for more than twenty-five years that her orthodox religion was not able to satisfy. She finally found several mystical groups that taught reincarnation and karma. She could comprehend and accept these concepts despite her strong religious training. Soon thereafter, she joined Eckankar.

The third ECKist had always found himself an outsider. He enjoyed church as a boy, but only because his duties as an altar boy allowed him to sit not in the congregation, but off on the side with the other altar boys. When he grew up, he accomplished his dream of earning a huge sum of money so that finances were of little concern. That goal accomplished, he realized there must be more to life and started the search that eventually led to Eckankar.

The psychologist wanted to know one more thing.

"I understand why you joined Eckankar," he said, "but what need does it fulfill now to keep you here?"

"For instance," he continued, "suppose that a man were starving. Yet he knows that food is to be found in a certain place. This need to satisfy his hunger drives him onward until he finds the food and eats to his heart's content.

"If someone then offered him ten dollars to eat another heaping plateful of food he would refuse, since he is no longer hungry."

"So I want to know," said the psychologist, "what keeps you in Eckankar now that your initial need has been fulfilled?"

All three of them answered that they were in contact with the ECK, or Spirit. They found Its twin aspects of the Light and Sound in their inner lives during the Spiritual Exercises of ECK. Many times also, they met with the Inner Master. This contact with the ECK was their life force. Without It they became restless and dead.

Each time they achieved one goal, the Inner Master set them another so they could unfold further. If they neglected to meet the challenge, the inner communication dried up. This left them hollow inside.

The third ECKist expressed it this way: "I have found this inner nudging directs my life better than I can myself."

Another said, "It tells me when I've been eating too much and had better slack off because my congested body needs time to clean itself—or get sick."

The lady found that It gave her insights into her own future as well as into daily problems.

The psychologist learned answers he hardly expected. It was fortunate he did not interview Richard, who so easily predicted the ice cream farewell party. That would surely have strained his belief.

40

Discoveries Beyond

Periodically, to satisfy my curiosity, I ask people in ECK what they originally found attractive about Eckankar.

For me it had been the freedom to move about with Soul Travel. Soul Travel allowed me to rise above the restrictions of military duties that sent me two years overseas, away from my family, and allowed me to visit the farm I loved.

Surprising to me, other ECKists said they felt an overpowering need for love, and this is why they follow Eckankar today.

For centuries, the Living ECK Master has passed along to individuals the secret knowledge that lies behind questions such as "What is life all about? Have I lived before? What is beyond death?"

The old saying, "When the seeker is ready, the master appears," holds true even today. One lady said she had *In My Soul I Am Free*, the biography of Paul Twitchell by Brad Steiger, on her bedroom dresser for two years before finally finishing it. She read half, then set it aside for later.

A wide variety of paperbacks flowed across her dresser over the next two years before she picked it up again. Most of the other books she gave to friends. This particular one, however, stayed in her bedroom. She dusted around it every week and often wondered what to do with it, but it remained.

Two years later she found Paul Twitchell's *ECKANKAR, The Key to Secret Worlds*. Some inner urging, no doubt, prompted her to buy it. She read it from cover to cover, then remembered the book on top of her dresser. After a delay of two years, she finally read it completely through.

Another young man confided that he entered a bookstore intending to shoplift a book just for the fun of it. He swiped *The Tiger's Fang*, the story of Paul Twitchell's own journey to God-Realization.

An inner knowingness clicked inside the shoplifter: "This is it!" He returned to the store, paid for the book and bought another in order to learn more about Eckankar.

"What is beyond death?" is a question that has perplexed man down through the ages. A gentleman I know personally had an out-of-the-body experience in his early forties. A heart attack struck him down and the ambulance rushed him to the hospital. The doctors worked frantically to save his life.

In the meantime, the sick man had left the body and was hovering near the ceiling like a pair of eyes. He felt great happiness and no concern at all about the fate of his pale physical body stretched out on the operating table. A doctor injected a powerful drug, and the victim felt himself drawn back to his body. He had no desire, however, to return to it.

Later, when he had recovered enough to speak, he related to the nurse what had happened in the operating room while he lay unconscious. Nobody would believe his story. Finally, he deemed it wise to

200

keep this experience to himself, because the medical staff feared his mind had been damaged by the lack of oxygen.

A friend of mine related a similar story about his dad. When they were still children, his father told them about the serious illness that had brought him to the hospital in critical condition. The father told his children this story so that they would not go through life fearing death.

His heart had stopped and the medical doctor tried in vain to start it up again. This happened many years ago before the medical knowledge advanced to where it is today.

The family vet was also present. He pounded both his fists on the stricken man's chest, trying to restore his heartbeat.

The father, in the meantime, was outside his body, watching the frantic efforts of the two doctors below. The father was concerned with happier matters. When his heart had stopped, he found himself walking up a spiral staircase. Enchanting melodies pulled him along, ever further up the stairs. He wished never to return. Abruptly, he faced a doorway. He knew instinctively that if he passed through it, his earthly life would be ended. That suited him fine, and he started eagerly toward the door.

At that moment, the veterinarian pounded his chest with even sharper blows. This infuriated the father as he was slowly drawn away from the doorway that led into the heavenly, blissful life. He awoke, shouting curses. The doctors and nurses supposed that he was delirious, but he was furious simply because they had reactivated his heartbeat. Consequently, he claimed to have lost all fear of death—after he settled down somewhat.

One of the doctors had lost his pen during the excitement. When the father told the nurse what he had seen while his body lingered near death, she would not believe him. Imagine her shock when he told her where to recover the pen. No one dared believe his tale, yet they could not explain how he knew where to find the lost pen.

Although the father is not a member of Eckankar, his son, who told the story, has been a member for several years. "My dad isn't a member," he said, "but as far as he's concerned, Eckankar makes more sense than a lot of that other stuff."

Both of the men who had the opportunity to be outside the physical body and return to it are strong individuals, untroubled by orthodox fears of guilt and sin. They know they stand completely responsible for everything they do. Nor do they tremble when somebody tries to make them join one religious organization or another with the threat: "Join us or go to hell." In early American lingo, these two are among many others who have been "across the creek and over the mountain."

Each person must find his own way in life, and at his own pace.

41

Long Distance

My wife's mother is not a member of Eckankar, yet she knows how to contact the ECK, or Spirit, to help her resolve her everyday problems. She calls my wife.

My wife always tells her, "Mom, I just give it to the ECK and the Living ECK Master. I don't do anything myself." Her mother could do it directly, too, but she sometimes lacks confidence in exercising her right to contact Spirit.

Her mother once opened a small restaurant in her town. It was not long before mealtime found her place packed with workmen who just loved her homemade pies. Despite all the apparent business, the cash register did not jingle the way she expected. She was barely making ends meet.

She called my wife and told her about the situation. "Would you please mention this to the Living ECK Master the next time you see him, please?"

Mom did not realize it was not necessary to tell him about her problem. It was enough just to call upon Spirit to resolve the problem. The Living ECK Master does not have the time to physically answer every request made for help. But the ECK begins working, for instance, the moment a letter to him is dropped into the mailbox.

Mom's way to call upon Spirit seems to be by calling her daughter. Shortly thereafter, she found that the cook was dipping into the till. After she fired him, her restaurant started to thrive again.

On another occasion, one of her small grandsons got very sick. The child was only three months old and his bowels locked. Mom got the intuitive feeling that the boy was allergic to his mother's milk, but the mother would not believe it. She continued to breast-feed him, and the child continued to lose vitality.

My wife's mom called up and told what she suspected about the child's allergy. The next day the mother's milk dried up. The baby had to be put on another formula and quickly recovered.

My wife knows that she is not doing anything miraculous. Her mother's technique to contact this all-seeing, all-knowing ECK is calling my wife.

Much is made today about the miracles performed by Jesus, yet he never took personal credit for them. When questioned about miraculous events, he said, "It is not I that do these things, but my Father in heaven." He was referring to this divine Spirit.

The great Tibetan ECK Master, Rebazar Tarzs, told Paul Twitchell this in *The Far Country*: "All miracles are but the play of mind. They are not the operations of any divine power, as most people believe."

The Living ECK Master also discounts any special abilities. He will answer on this order: "I am merely a vehicle for the ECK."

There have been several instances when I became very ill. During the Spiritual Exercises of

ECK in the evening, I was quite surprised to hear the sound of a vibration like a fast-running motor. At the same time, I moved out of the physical body into the Soul body. Several invisible individuals directed this Sound Current of the ECK to the part of my body causing the distress.

Healing is usually a matter of adjusting the vibrations of the affected area to harmonize with those of the rest of the body. When the body's parts are all moving at the proper rate again, then the physical member recovers its health.

But healing does not come just because I ask. Sometimes I must go to the dentist because I have allowed a condition to get too far out of harmony, and it must be repaired in a down-to-earth way. That is the way certain karma is worked off.

The Living ECK Master hooks up the individual with the ECK, the Audible Life Current, when the time is right. When this occurs, then the person benefits from the direct intervention in his life by this supreme spiritual force, the ECK.

Mom, however, prefers to get her answers long distance.

42

Meeting the Master

The time comes eventually when the chela has earned the right to meet the Master. Nothing can keep them apart. In fact, it is a spiritual law that when the seeker is ready, then the Master appears.

All kinds of imaginary obstacles may confront the chela when he nears this point, but the force of the ECK brings him ever closer to the Master. At a seminar I once met a man who said he had seen the Inner Master and now wished to meet the Living ECK Master, too. After one of the Master's evening talks, the man went to shake his hand.

The crowd was heavy as the Master approached. The man appeared to be directly in the path where he could put out his hand as the Master came by.

Just then a woman beside him dropped her purse. The people were massed so tightly together that she could not bend down to retrieve it. At the same moment, the Master moved further away. The man was caught in a predicament. Should he pick up the purse and chance missing the meeting with the Master, or should he not help the woman find her purse?

He stooped over to help find the purse, resigned

to greeting the Master personally another time. The woman thanked him, but by now the Master was far out of reach.

Just when all seemed lost, the Master stopped, turned around and stretched back over the wall of people to shake his hand. The chela had won, but only because he was first willing to give of himself to another. This is one of the requirements of Soul on Its spiritual journey to the high God planes.

The ability to See, Know and Be, the marks of a spiritual adept, are outstanding in the Living ECK Master. Often this shows up in subtle ways, left up to the consciousness of the chela to understand how much the Master really knows or does not know.

During my first few seminars, I felt an overpowering urgency to meet with Paul at each seminar. But as the seminars got larger, it became harder for Paul to meet with the growing number of people. I found that I was being selfish by always standing in the receiving line, depriving another who had not yet met him the opportunity to do so.

Paul left the lecture room surrounded by the ever-present crowd wishing to meet him and shake his hand. I had already met him several times and realized it was time to step back and give somebody else the chance.

I moved off quietly by myself and sat on a table that stood against the wall. The Master and the crowd flowed past me slowly like a river that I remembered from my childhood. I enjoyed the freedom to sit, for once, on the outside.

It was most pleasant to watch the chelas meet the Master. Paul stopped then, and turned to look directly at me with a long, steady gaze. So long, in fact, that I started to squirm with embarrassment because his look said: "It is no longer necessary to meet with me every time in the physical. You have learned the secret of how to meet with me in the Soul body."

The pure love of the Master can at other times be too strong for the chela, who does not yet know how to handle it within his worlds. The ECK comes through the Living ECK Master in powerful waves, yet the student learns how to regulate this flow within himself. The Inner Master teaches him how to do it.

A friend of mine was allowed to sit in with Paul and the Eckankar Board of Trustees during one of their meetings shortly before Paul translated. On the table stood a vase of twelve red roses. At the end of the meeting, Paul gave one of the roses to each of the people present.

The rose was a gift of the Master. A funny thing about such a spiritual gift is that you cannot hoard it for yourself. It must be passed on, because it is a gift of love.

My friend gave her rose to me. I felt about ten feet tall and wanted to wear it in my lapel until it dropped its last petal.

The seminar over, I went down to the bus station to catch a bus home. A grandmother and her grandchild sat in the seat in front of me. The little girl was sweet, quiet, and minding her manners among all the doting passengers. She looked back over the seat and saw the rose in my lapel and wanted it. I gave it to her.

Amazingly, the child changed to a spoiled brat. She screamed, fussed, and cried, pulled the petals off the stem one by one, until the grandmother gave her a good, sound spanking.

I saw that the presence of the Master, even through a rose, can produce starling changes in people. The karma speeds up and the rough edges of Soul are polished more quickly so that It may one day also become a Co-worker with God.

It is possible to meet with the Master in ways much more sublime than in person. The gift of a rose from the Master passed along from chela to chela may also stir up the spiritual currents of Soul, no matter how young the body within which It resides, and whether or not It has ever heard about Eckankar.

43

Saint and Seekers

My wife met a young lady in the bookstore of a community college. The woman was looking through the books and said with some surprise, "Do you realize there aren't any books on Christianity?"

It was true. The shelves bulged with textbooks on the many different kinds of philosophies and isms, but hardly one on Christianity.

"I'm going to have a baby again," the redhead confided. "Every time that happens, I get religious."

She complained that other groups attacked Christianity because nobody who was a Christian meditated. "That's not true," she fumed. "Look at all the nuns and monks."

She wanted to find a book about the Christian saints. My wife assured her, "Of course, the Christians had a lot of saints who meditated. There was Padre Pio for one, the Italian Capuchin monk; St. Therese of France; St. Francis Xavier, the sixteenth-century Spanish saint; St. Anthony of Padua, and a host of others."

My wife told her about *ECKANKAR, The Key to Secret Worlds* by Paul Twitchell and the chapter, "Unique Case Histories of Soul Travelers."

"You might also want to read a little book called *The Practice of the Presence of God* by Brother Lawrence," she continued.

In the year 1666, Nicholas Herman of French Lorraine joined the barefooted Carmelites in Paris. He became known as Brother Lawrence. In every simple taks of life, he tried to walk in the presence of God. His job was scrubbing the pots and pans in the monastery, yet he never complained. The little book is a testimony to a humble man overlooked by the masses who desire a spectacular saint for an idol.

There is no need to seclude oneself in a modern monastery in order to find God. A number of individuals are on the same quest for God-Realization today, responsible members of the community who hold down jobs and support their families.

Likely, they reflect a higher order of sainthood than that which requires others to bathe and support them while they selfishly dribble their lives away in meditation.

Perhaps Charles is one such person who is a member of that higher order of modern-day saints. In 1969, he was driving down a main street in San Diego. The traffic light turned green, but his eye was captured by the face of a man on a large poster tacked to a light pole on the street corner.

The cars behind him honked their horns for him to move along. He was blocking traffic. Charles forgot about the sign and the haunting face until several years later when he encountered the face again under different circumstances.

Late one night, in his bedroom, three strangers suddenly appeared at the foot of his bed. One of them was Caucasian, and he was dressed in conventional street clothes. The other two wore long robes.

They all looked sternly at him, then disappeared as mysteriously as they had come.

A few days later, Charles bought *Herbs: the Magic Healers* and *The Tiger's Fang* by Paul Twitchell. On the back of one book was the picture of the man he had seen in his room and on the poster. It was that of Paul Twitchell, the leader of Eckankar at that time. His mind flashed back several years to the traffic intersection where he had held up traffic in order to get a better look at the face on the poster.

Charles noted that there was a rash of the "stranger in the bedroom " sightings going around. Several close friends also received these visits.

The spiritual travelers dropped in at the home of one particular acquaintance who had repeatedly warned Charles to forgo his study into the spiritual mysteries. Their visit, however, convinced his friend there might indeed be substance to the claim that such Soul Travelers did really exist in modern times. A quieter meeting with Eckankar was reported by a woman named Terri. Terri never felt an overpowering urge to "find that missing something in life." She was, however, mildly interested in reincarnation.

She found herself in a bookstore near her home in Syracuse, New York. None of the book titles interested her especially until her glance fell upon *In My Soul I Am Free* by Brad Steiger.

Reading halfway through it, she knew this was what she wanted. She sent to the publisher for more information and took the information in stride, keeping her balanced outlook.

Jerry's experiences with the spiritual life were more dramatic. He encountered Paul Twitchell twenty years before Paul brought Eckankar out into the mainstream of the twentieth century in 1965.

Their meetings, however, were in the spiritual worlds via Soul Travel. Jerry often wondered who this little man might be with the baggy trousers. Every time he came, he took Jerry out of the body into the heavenly worlds.

One time, overcome with curiosity, Jerry asked the gentle, little man, "Say, you aren't the Angel of Death, are you?" Paul just rolled with laughter.

Later, Jerry decided that the spiritual traveler who took him into the other worlds was really the "Angel of Life." He had never met anyone before who could actually take him to the different heavens.

Nevertheless, during all those years, Jerry's meetings with his unnamed friend occurred only in the non-material realms. This changed dramatically when his dad was dying of a terminal illness. Jerry visited his father in the hospital. Downstairs in the bookstore, he saw a paperback with a face on the cover that looked familiar. The man turned out to be Paul Twitchell, his mysterious visitor for twenty years. This was the first time he knew the identity of the stranger.

Paul Twitchell translated (died) in 1971. Jerry saw him once more on the inner planes. This time Paul looked at him and waved his hand in farewell. A new guide came into Jerry's life. Paul turned him over to the new Living ECK Master.

"Paul's parting wave," recounts Jerry, "was just the way it's pictured in the film *ECKANKAR, A Way of Life.*

None of the people mentioned in this chapter fit the common mold of saints. If sainthood implies "near perfection," then you can count these candidates out of the running.

The Living ECK Master points out to each person on the Path to God that there is no final heaven, there is no final state of perfection that any person can claim like a merit badge. There is always one more step.

That is an awesome goal for any Seeker of Life.

44

Promises in Japan

Several times I have heard ECK Masters say, "We make no promises." What does that mean? Have you ever read any of Louis L'Amour's Western novels? His stories are historically accurate so that if a hundred and fifty years from now someone says, "I wonder what the Old West was really like?" he will find a true picture in the Louis L'Amour Westerns.

In those early frontier days, a man's future was only as good as his word. If he shook hands on a contract, that was better than any legal contract today. Any man who broke his word lost his credit in town. Nobody would do business with him. In fact, somebody generally told him right out, "You'd better move along. You're going to starve here." A man's word was all he had—or needed.

The Air Force had taught me not to put undue trust in promises. While I was still stationed at a remote air base in Japan, on the northern end of Honshu Island, it was early autumn and the bleak prospect of the severe winter of that region was not far away. Off to the west, on the distant mountain peaks, we could see snow. An airman who had been

217

here last winter advised, "When you see the snow on the peaks, you have a month before it comes down here. Dress warm!"

Good fortune seemed to be smiling upon me, however. Just about then, word came down through the military chain of command about a new air station authorized to open down south near Tokyo. This was a plush assignment, since the winters were mild there just like in southern California.

Sixty airmen were on the original list to transfer south. Nobody relished the harsh winter that was just around the corner. I was on the list, too.

My sergeant said, "Well, how do you feel about going to Tokyo?"

"I'll believe it when I see it," I answered. I imagine I had seen too many promises dashed to pieces during my many lives here on the physical plane. At any rate, I lived moment-to-moment.

A week later, a new list was posted. About twenty airmen had been cut from the transfer roster. Somebody said that the funds had been cut back. My name was still on the list, but several friends found theirs gone.

"Well, you're still on," said Sergeant Hardy. "I don't think they'll cut back any more."

"I'll believe it when I see it."

Sergeant Hardy was amused by my hard-nosed attitude. It seemed inconceivable that the transfer program could get cut again. Nevertheless, next week another abbreviated list passed through the squadron. This continued for several weeks. Each list dropped a few more airmen until only eight of us first term airmen remained.

We were standing out on the runway, all eight of us, gear fully packed, waiting to board the cargo plane for Tokyo. The word had gotten around the squadron about the airman whose only reaction to this glorious assignment was a consistent, "I'll believe it when I see it."

"Do you believe it now?" asked one of the remaining airmen as we watched one of the four engines start to crank up.

"Wait until we're gone, then I'll tell you."

The C-130 shuddered as two more engines turned over and caught. The fourth one, unfortunately, remained silent. So did our group. They looked at me with new respect, the joking gone from their lips. As long as we remained on the ground, there was always time for a courier to roar up in a jeep with canceled orders. Snow flurries whipped the runway as we glumly viewed the possibility of still spending a bleak and miserable winter here.

The cargo plane never did take off that morning. We finally transferred by military vehicle to the Japanese train station and loaded aboard a civilian passenger train. Many dreary hours later found us walking into our new barracks at the air station near Tokyo. The eight of us were all that remained of the original sixty airmen who formerly were to come here. We were a fortunate lot.

One of the airmen looked at me and said, "You've got to believe it now—you can see it!"

"You're right," I agreed, "I believe it."

Maybe that is what the ECK Masters meant about promises, too.

45

The Reporter

What can one expect when he moves his consciousness via Soul Travel into the invisible planes while his physical body sleeps?

Sometimes I have encountered the twin aspects of the ECK, Spirit, in the Sound and Light during Soul Travel. A lot of other times, however, I find myself on the inner planes serving and working with the people who live there. Often, the situation is humble. The story of *The Reporter* is a report of one such occasion.

* * *

I was a newspaper reporter. I had been watching an old man of eighty summers who stood outside a grocery store in a New England town.

The streets were icy and slippery with snow, and the old man walked carefully along the street to his room. I thought, "Here might be a story." Perhaps the old man was a former seafarer, now grown old and forgotten, awaiting his time to leave this earth.

He was an elusive old man. Nor did he walk with a shaky step as I had imagined he should. At times he walked slowly, yet at other times he stalked along the pavement with the steps of youth.

The old man walked along the street, a lady behind him. She walked with loud, clacking heels. When she got near, he stepped to the side and let her go by, the way old people sometimes do. He turned his back to her as she passed, so that she never glimpsed his face. I had followed quietly behind her but stopped beside him. He glanced up with surprise as he saw me standing there.

"Finally, I got you!" I said to the old gentleman.

He smiled a little and continued on his way. I had to speed up to keep pace with him. He said he did not have much to offer a guest, but I could come home.

So we moved steadily along the street, turned up an alley and climbed rickety old stairs. The Atlantic Ocean was pounding on the beach just a few yards away.

He leaned out of the window and threw the fluffy little rabbit to the children, and they all laughed.

We entered a little room. He immediately went back into another room. The front room, I noticed, had another exit down a back flight of stairs. The door fit the frame poorly. I tried without success to shut it against the cold, wintry wind.

In the living room, I found him near the open window. He was a broad-shouldered man, dressed in a flame red woolen shirt. His tattered tan overcoat hung in a small closet with the door ajar. He looked a lot stronger and healthier now than he had on the street in front of the grocery store in his threadbare overcoat.

He peered out of the window, watching the children playing in the street. He watched them for a while, then shouted out with a hearty voice reminiscent of a seafaring man of years long gone, "Hey, do you want to see the rabbit?"

The children's voices chorused back, "Yes, let's see the rabbit! We want to see the rabbit!"

Then, unexpectedly, he asked me, "Do you see the rabbit?"

I peeked over the edge of the window sill, down to the pavement below. I could not see a rabbit and told him so.

"Well, maybe you aren't looking carefully enough," he said. Then he walked away from the window and came back a moment later with a little toy rabbit made out of cotton in his hand. Cutely dressed, it had two long ears, white fur, and a red jacket that matched the warmth of his own flaming shirt.

He leaned out of the window and threw the fluffy little rabbit to the children, and they all laughed. This seemed to be a common occasion, the children looking up to the window and seeing this little rabbit floating down whenever the old man could offer a new one.

The toy rabbits became treasures for the children lucky enough to catch one. The rabbits were something warm and soft, happy and bright in the midst of the cold, hard asphalt. They were the little spark of life lacking in their harsh playground.

Suddenly, footsteps pounded up the stairway. A short, fat woman burst through the door. She was furious. She shook a fist as she charged into the room. In her other hand, she held the rabbit.

"Here's the rabbit!" she screamed. "I suppose now I should sign for it to prove that my child didn't steal it!"

She called the old man a meddling fool. She added a lot of other unsavory things. I sat there quietly, embarrassed and ashamed, not quite knowing how to handle her outrage.

The old man stepped into the other room for a moment, and I confronted her, defending the old man. I told her that he was giving away the rabbits out of love from his heart, because he knew that children need something happy in their life. He certainly did not expect to sign a receipt for every little rabbit that he gave away. It was a gift of love.

The woman quieted down when she heard this, feeling somewhat embarrassed herself. She cried, regretting her foolish behavior. I put my arm around her shoulder. The rolls of fat convulsed as she sobbed, because it had been a long time for her, too, since she had grown up on the pavement below. She had never had these little specks of life—the little toy rabbits—and so had not understood the old man's generosity.

After the fat lady had left, the door reopened.

This old man, whom I had supposed was lonely, greeted a horde of people, each one bringing a little food already prepared. They put it all on the table—hot dishes and casseroles, milk, wine and beer.

In a few minutes, some of the women had set the table, and I was invited to eat. The food was humble, but there was plenty of it.

Somehow, I felt I had not earned my share. The old man looked at me with a twinkle in his eye. "Go on and eat! You stood up to her for me. Maybe next time she'll bring your share."

I knew then that the secret to his many friendships was his warm and loving heart. He enjoyed each moment of life.

* * *

The simplicity of this story reminds me of what the great Tibetan ECK Master, Rebazar Tarzs, said to Paul Twitchell in *Stranger by the River*. "Can you think of life to be more than what it is at this moment?"

46

The Mean, Old Billy Goat

One final note. HU is an ancient name for God long known to the ECK Masters of the Order of Vairagi. It is a spiritually charged word that ECKists find helpful when they want assistance in trouble. A friend told me the following story of what he learned about chanting HU.

* * *

Charlie lived on a farm in the South. One day he got an urgent telephone call from the wife of his neighbor, who was in his eighties.

"The bull's got him in a corner," she cried. "Can you please help him?"

Charlie, of course, ran right over. When he got there, he found the old gentleman trapped in a small space behind the water trough. The bull could not get in, but neither could Mr. Bates get out.

Charlie picked up a three-tined pitchfork and pricked the bull's hide until it backed away. In the meantime, while Charlie held off the bull, he called to Mr. Bates to see if he had safely escaped, but he was careful not to take his eyes from the bull.

"Are you all right, Mr. Bates?"

The old man did not answer. Had the excitement given him a heart attack? Charlie chanced a glance from the bull to the trough.

Mr. Bates was gone. He had slipped out safely and was even now stomping off to the house, determined to call the cattle shipper and sell his dangerous bull.

Charlie had turned his head for only one instant. Just that quickly, however, the bull had tossed his horns and sent the fork flying from his hands. Charlie made a mad scramble for the tiny niche of safety behind the water trough. The bull snorted and threw dirt with his hooves outside the entrance, being too big to get in.

Charlie now found himself trapped in the same spot from which he had just rescued Mr. Bates. What to do?

Charlie now found himself trapped in the same spot from which he had just rescued Mr. Bates. What to do?

Charlie began to chant HU, knowing it carried the power to change his predicament if it was the will of the ECK, Spirit.

"For a minute or so," Charlie said, "nothing happened. I wondered if I should keep chanting or call for help. The only trouble, the house was too far away for anyone to hear me."

Continuing to chant HU, Charlie then noticed a mean, old billy goat getting agitated in the same fence as the bull. The goat cocked his head, lowered his massive horns and charged full speed into the soft stomach of the enraged bull.

The goat's attack interested the bull, since it knocked the wind clear out of him. The last Charlie saw of the bull was when it stormed off after the billy goat. The goat scampered to safety, too, leaving the bull with no entertainment for all his trouble.

Charlie could not decide if chanting HU had helped or not. Perhaps the goat's attack was a coincidence. Nevertheless, Charlie was delighted to have escaped the horns of the bull. Should the bull have been so lucky with the goat!

HU can be sung as "Hugh," the English name, or spelled out in a long, drawn-out chant with first the "H," then the "U."

Someday, perhaps, the reader will try out the power of HU for himself. Unless, of course, a mean, old billy goat will do just as well!

How to Study ECK Further

People want to know the secrets of life and death. In response to this need Sri Harold Klemp, today's spiritual leader of Eckankar, and Paul Twitchell, its modern-day founder, have written special monthly discourses which reveal the Spiritual Exercises of ECK—to lead Soul in a direct way to God.

Those who wish to study Eckankar can receive these special monthly discourses which give clear, simple instructions for the spiritual exercises. The first annual series of discourses is *The ECK Dream Discourses*. Mailed each month, the discourses will offer insight into your dreams and what they mean to you.

The techniques in these discourses, when practiced twenty minutes a day, are likely to prove survival beyond death. Many have used them as a direct route to Self-Realization, where one learns his mission in life. The next stage, God Consciousness, is the joyful state wherein Soul becomes the spiritual traveler, an agent for God. The underlying principle one learns is this: Soul exists because God loves It.

Study of ECKANKAR includes:

1. Twelve monthly lessons of *The ECK Dream Discourses,* which include these titles: "Dreams—The Bridge to Heaven," "The Dream Master," "How to Interpret Your Dreams," "Dream Travel to Soul Travel," and more. You may study them alone at home or in a class with others.
2. The *Mystic World,* a quarterly newsletter with a Wisdom Note and articles by the Living ECK Master. In it are also letters and articles from students of Eckankar around the world.
3. Special mailings to keep you informed of upcoming Eckankar seminars and activities around the world, new study materials available from Eckankar, and more.
4. The opportunity to attend ECK Satsang classes and book discussions with others in your community.
5. Initiation eligibility.
6. Attendance at certain chela meetings at ECK seminars.

How to Find Out More:

Call **(612) 544-0066,** Monday through Friday, 8 a.m. to 5 p.m. central time, to find out more about how to study *The ECK Dream Discourses,* or use the coupon at the back of this book. Or write: **ECKANKAR, Att: ECK Study, P.O. Box 27300, Minneapolis, MN 55427 U.S.A.**

Introductory Books on ECKANKAR

The Book of ECK Parables, Volume One,
Harold Klemp

Learn how to find spiritual fulfillment in everyday life from this series of over ninety light, easy-reading stories by Eckankar's spiritual leader, Sri Harold Klemp. The parables reveal secrets of Soul Travel, dreams, karma, health, reincarnation, and—most important of all—initiation into the Sound and Light of God, in everyday settings we can understand.

ECKANKAR—The Key to Secret Worlds,
Paul Twitchell

Paul Twitchell, modern-day founder of Eckankar, gives you the basics of this ancient teaching. Includes six specific Soul Travel exercises to see the Light and hear the Sound of God, plus case histories of Soul Travel. Learn to recognize yourself as Soul—and journey into the heavens of the Far Country.

The Wind of Change, Harold Klemp

What are the hidden spiritual reasons behind every event in your life? With stories drawn from his own lifelong training, Eckankar's spiritual leader shows you how to use the power of Spirit to discover those reasons. Follow him from the Wisconsin farm of his youth, to a military base in Japan; from a job in Texas, into the realms beyond, as he shares the secrets of Eckankar.

The Tiger's Fang, Paul Twitchell

Paul Twitchell's teacher, Rebazar Tarzs, takes him on a journey through vast worlds of Light and Sound, to sit at the feet of the spiritual Masters. Their conversations bring out the secret of how to draw closer to God—and awaken Soul to Its spiritual destiny. Many have used this book, with its vivid descriptions of heavenly worlds and citizens, to begin their own spiritual adventures.

For more information about the books and teachings of Eckankar, please write: **ECKANKAR, Att: Information, P.O. Box 27300, Minneapolis, MN 55427 U.S.A.**

Or look under **ECKANKAR** in your local phone book for an Eckankar Center near you.

There May Be an
ECKANKAR Study Group near You

Eckankar offers a variety of local and international activities for the spiritual seeker. With hundreds of study groups worldwide, Eckankar is near you! Many areas have Eckankar Centers where you can browse through the books in a quiet, unpressured environment, talk with others who share an interest in this ancient teaching, and attend beginning discussion classes on how to gain the attributes of Soul: wisdom, power, love, and freedom.

Around the world, Eckankar study groups offer special one-day or weekend seminars on the basic teachings of Eckankar. Check your phone book under **ECKANKAR**, or call **(612) 544-0066** for membership information and the location of the Eckankar Center or study group nearest you. Or write **ECKANKAR, Att: Information, P.O. Box 27300, Minneapolis, MN 55427 U.S.A.**

☐ Please send me information on the nearest Eckankar discussion or study group in my area.

☐ I would like an application form to study Eckankar further. Please send me more information about the twelve-month Eckankar study discourses on dreams.

Please type or print clearly   941

Name _____

Street _____ Apt. # _____

City _____ State/Prov. _____

Zip/Postal Code _____ Country _____

(Our policy: Your name and address are held in strict confidence. We do not rent or sell our mailing lists. Nor will anyone call on you. Our purpose is only to show people the ECK way home to God.)

Eckankar, Att: Information, P.O. Box 27300, Minneapolis, MN 55427, U.S.A.